THE WALLS OF JERUSA

RONNIE ELLENBLUM   AMNON RAMON

THE WALLS OF JERUSALEM

A guide to the ramparts walking tour

 YAD IZHAK BEN-ZVI • JERUSALEM

Cover design: Mike Horton

ISBN 965-217-122-0

CONTENTS

Upon the initiative of East Jerusalem Development Ltd. and the Rachel Yanait Ben-Zvi Youth Education Center, Ronnie Ellenblum prepared a guide to the Ramparts Walk, which was published in Hebrew in 1988. *Walls of Jerusalem* is an English version, revised and updated by Amnon Ramon. Publication was made possible by the generosity of David B. Hermelin; Michael, Daniel and Sara Lipson, Sol Kirschner; John and Shirley Graham, all of the USA, and Dr. Helga Kronheim of Israel.

We express our gratitude to Yitzhak Yaakovy and Sara Malka of East Jerusalem Development Ltd. for their ongoing encouragement and assistance; to Professor Yehoshua Ben-Arieh, Dr. Dan Bahat and Gadi Wexler for their helpful suggestions and comments; and to Tamar Sofer who produced the maps.

FOREWORD

If this is your first visit to Jerusalem, you most likely have expectations of religious sites, places of historical and archeological significance, and bustling oriental bazaars. Apparently, most visitors to Jerusalem have preconceptions of Jerusalem's Old City. But by the time that your first visit to the Old City is over, your own special Jerusalem will have taken shape.

There are Jerusalemites — 'locals' for whom the Old City is mainly a conglomeration of streets and market places overflowing with merchandise. Others relate to specific places in the Old City and rejoice in the opening of each 'new' archeological site. For many Jews, the Old City is the route to the Western Wall, so close to the Temple Mount. Christian pilgrims have their own special routes leading them to 'their' holy places. For Moslems, the two holiest sites in the city are al-Aqsa and the Dome of the Rock mosques. Each one of these visitors is convinced that he knows Jerusalem and that the Old City is what he imagines it to be. The wall surrounding the Old City certainly adds to this impression, conveying a sense of consolidated uniformity. From wherever we look at the Old City we gain the same impression: walls of a similar height and pattern built of Jerusalem stone and capped with crenellated sections. The towers projecting from the wall are of equal height and form, so that the city gates become the main landmarks.

The Ottoman Turkish engineers who constructed the walls in the first half of the sixteenth century performed their task ably. Even pre-existing sections incorporated into the Turkish wall in no way affected its uniform appearance, which has remained unchanged for over 400 years.

But the impression of unity will be contradicted if we enter the Old City several times, each one by a different gate. Only then does it become apparent that the beneath the facade of uniformity lie hidden surprises. Behind each gate one finds distinctive colors, aromas, dress, languages, foods; at times even the light refracts differently in the city's various quarters. Few places in the world stimulate the senses of its visitor with such a variety of experiences.

7

Jerusalem surrounded by walls   This guide proposes a different way of seeing Jerusalem: *a tour atop the city walls,* giving the visitor a bird's-eye view of the city in just a few short hours. This 'Ramparts Walk' leads us among private houses, courtyards, churches and public institutions; from the wall we can watch the crowds making their way through the gates, glance at hidden corners, view spectacular landscapes and come to know the city from a very special vantage point, revealing its many facets from above.

Before setting out, we recommend that you wander around the area inside the gates and through the adjacent plazas, drink a cup of steaming hot coffee in one of the tiny coffee houses and watch the crowd go by.

A city of quarters   A congeries of languages, nationalities, occupations, dress, smells and sounds will engulf you as you enter the Old City. There is no single central square uniting its various quarters. Rather, each of its neighborhoods contains its own central plaza, reflecting the special character of that quarter. The Armenian Quarter's square is concealed by its walls. It is generally empty, characteristic of Old Jerusalem's small Armenian community. The two squares of the Jewish Quarter blend the old and new, giving expression to the renewal of the Jewish community in the Old City. The Christian Quarter has no central plaza, but the courtyard in front of the Church of the Holy Sepulcher serves that purpose to a certain extent; the ceremonies, dress, languages and tourists that fill it continuously express, perhaps more than anything else, the international, ecumenical character of this Quarter. The expansive esplanade of Haram al-Sharif (the Temple Mount) is where the Moslem inhabitants of Jerusalem congregate. You can always find people there: faithful believers making their way to prayer or study, schoolchildren repeating their lessons as they walk, people just lounging about, villagers who have come to visit the holy sites and — like everywhere else in the city — tourists and other visitors.

The squares adjoining the city's gates are where people mingle daily: young and old, Jews and Moslems, Christians and Greek Orthodox, Catholics, Armenians, Copts and Ethiopians, Lutherans and Anglicans, tourists and pilgrims of all ages, from all parts of the world. They are greeted by merchants plying their wares, vendors of carpets and souvenirs, shoe-shine boys, and salesmen of clothes. If you linger a bit you can inhale the fragrance of the freshly-baked *ka'ak* (an Arab bagel) sprinkled with sesame seeds and spiced with *za'atar* (cumin seeds with salt). Don't miss the *sahlab,* a hot, sweet, whitish oriental drink prepared from special roots and garnished with cinnamon and nuts, poured into a gleaming copper cup which keeps it warm. If you are touring in summer we suggest you try *tamarhandi,* an oriental drink prepared from dates and poured from a fascinating vessel carried on the vendor's back. Money changers, sellers of sweetmeats — all these are a mere foretaste of things to come at the end of the tour, when you wander through the markets. Jerusalem's markets, however, are hardly the place in which to sit back comfortably and watch the world go by. That's what the squares are for. And so we begin our tour with them.

The city wall contains seven gates facing all four points of the compass — the Jaffa Gate faces west; the New Gate, the Damascus Gate and Herod's Gate face north; the Lions' Gate faces east; the Zion Gate and the Dung Gate face south. All were originally built at an angle so as to prevent forced entry directly into the city.

SOME PRACTICAL INFORMATION

This guide offers you two walking tours. The *first* will lead you from Jaffa Gate to Damascus Gate and from there to the Lions' Gate—all in all about 2.1 km. and 2 to 3 hours at a leisurely pace. The *second* begins at the moat in front of the Citadel and ends at the Dung Gate, a walk of about 1.3 kilometers which should take you between 1 and 2 hours at a leisurely pace. They follow a paved path atop the Old City walls, reached by steps, and with a railing for your safety. The routes include suggested visits to three sites very near the ramparts: the Damascus Gate, the Citadel, and the archaeological excavations at the Ophel. To visit them you must pay an additional entrance fee.

Ascent and Descent There are three stations at which one may ascend or descend the wall: Jaffa Gate, the Citadel moat and Damascus Gate. There are five additional stations at which you may *only descend*: The New Gate, Herod's Gate, the Lions' Gate, the Dung Gate and Zion Gate. *Walking atop the walls is prohibited between the Dung Gate and the Lions' Gate.*

Tickets There is a charge for the Ramparts Walk. Tickets may be purchased at any of the three stations where one ascends the walls. The ticket is valid for two days, so that you are not obligated to do both walking tours on the same day.

Hours The Ramparts Walk is open every day (including Saturday) from 9 AM to 4 PM and on Friday and the eve of Jewish holidays from 9 AM to 2 PM.

Restrooms Restroom facilities along the route are at the Jerusalem Museum just within Jaffa Gate, at Damascus Gate just inside the walls, and near the Dung Gate.

Coffee Shops and Restaurants These may be found along your route just inside Jaffa Gate and Damascus Gate, as well as in the Jewish Quarter. To reach the latter descend at Zion Gate or the Dung Gate.

This guidebook provides full descriptions of the sites and views which you will meet as you walk atop the city walls. Many photos and maps have been added to make it easier for you to use the guide. Historical background material and explanations of terms used in the descriptions are in small print.

11

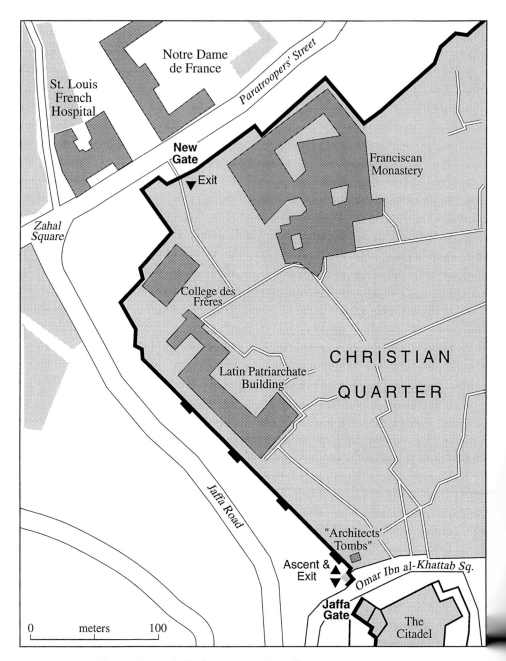

Map 1: From Jaffa Gate to the New Gate

12

PART ONE

From Jaffa Gate to the Lions' Gate

[Buses to Jaffa Gate: 3, 13, 19, 20, 30
Buses from the Dung Gate: 1, 2, 99]

Jaffa Gate Jaffa Gate is today the widest and major entrance to the Old City. Vehicles as well as pedestrians may use it. It is built on a natural ridge — to the south is the Valley of the Citadel and to the west the Hinnom Valley. Its topographical advantages explain why this gate has almost always served as the main entrance to the city.

There are three inscriptions in and around the gatehouse used by pedestrians: one is above the western entrance, the second inside the gatehouse and the most recent is outside the gate, above a stone bench upon which visitors can rest.

The main inscription, on the facade above the entrance, honors the Ottoman Sultan who built the city wall between 1537 and 1540, Suleiman bin Selim, known to Europeans as 'Suleiman the Magnificent'.

Suleiman's original reason for deciding to build the wall is not eniterly clear. Throughout the centuries prior to the Ottoman conquest, Jerusalem had no defensive wall. Many theories have been proposed to explain Suleiman's decision, such as the Turks' continued fear of the onslaught of further Crusades from Europe, or of attacks by marauding Beduin. The Ottoman Turks fought their battles with cannons, but the wall surrounding Jerusalem was not such that it could withstand cannon fire. The most logical explanation would thus appear to be that the city wall was erected as a defense measure against local marauders.

The gate was also called the Hebron Gate — Bab al-Khalil in Arabic, literally meaning 'The Gate of the Friend' (one of the names of the Patriarch Abraham was 'Friend of God'). This, of course, referred to Abraham's connection with the city of Hebron.

The second inscription, inside the gatehouse, is also devoted to Abraham: "There is no God except Allah, and Abraham is his beloved." In the past it was also known as 'Bethlehem Gate' and, during the Crusader period, 'David's Gate'.

13

The third inscription, outside the gate, refers to the completion of repairs to the wall after the Six-Day War: "On 10th of Teveth 5730 (December 19, 1969) the repairs to the city wall were completed," followed by a biblical quotation denoting the completion of the First Temple period walls by Nehemiah: "that we builded the wall of Jerusalem."

The section of the gate that guarded the entrance to the city until the end of the nineteenth century can still be seen. Until the 1870's the gates of Jerusalem were closed at sunset and opened the next morning at sunrise. They were also shut on Fridays at midday to allow Moslem soldiers to participate in prayer services. Jaffa Gate was the first to remain open at night, due to its proximity to the first neighborhoods built outside the city wall and also because it served as the terminus of the main road to Jaffa, which during the nineteenth century served as Jerusalem's port. The gate leads on to Jaffa Gate Square, referred to in Arabic as 'Omar Ibn al-Khattab Square', after the Caliph in whose reign, in 638, Jerusalem was conquered by the Moslems.

About twenty meters east of Jaffa Gate, to the left, is a small raised compound containing two tombs in the Ottoman style which local folklore associates with the construction of the city wall. According to a legend dating from the beginning of the eighteenth century, these are the graves of the two architects who designed the wall. They were executed because they failed to include Mt. Zion and the tomb of King David within Jerusalem's walled precinct; another version of the tale is that they lost their heads "so that they would not build a wall as magnificent as this elsewhere," or to prevent them from revealing the secrets of the wall to foreigners.

We now set out on the Ramparts Walk, reached by stairs to the left, a few meters before the 'Architects' Tombs'. We turn southwards to a balcony which overlooks 'Omar Ibn al-Khattab Square'.

The Citadel (Tower of David) From here we see the walls of the Citadel, surrounded by a shallow moat and above which, to the left, is a high tower; its lower section, built by Herod during the Second Temple period, has remained intact despite attacks upon it throughout the ages. Jerusalem's Christian rulers in the Byzantine period identified this tower with the Zion citadel mentioned in the Bible and therefore referred to it as 'The Tower of David', even though it is in no way connected with King David.

Jaffa Gate: Pedestrian entrance, with inscription above

Inscription dedicated to the Patriarch Abraham, next to Jaffa Gate

The road we see immediately below us was paved after the gate was no longer locked at night, and is associated with the visit of German Kaiser Wilhelm II to Jerusalem in 1898.

Kaiser Wilhelm's visit to Palestine was undoubtedly one of the most outstanding events in the country's history during the nineteenth century. In order to stress his pro-Turkish foreign policy, Wilhelm decided to pay a visit to the parts of the Ottoman Empire, including Istanbul. In order to achieve his imperialist aspirations of establishing overseas colonies like those of Great Britain and France, he constructed the second greatest naval fleet in the world and set out to conquer territories in Africa and Asia. He developed financial and commercial ties with the Ottoman Empire, and on October 31, 1898, visited Jerusalem. This was a landmark in the history of the Protestant Christian community in the Holy Land, for on that day the Kaiser consecrated the Protestant Church of the Redeemer inside the Old City and also laid the foundation stone of the Catholic Dormition Abbey, which we will see later in our tour.
The Ottoman authorities spared no effort to ensure that the visit would befit a royal personage. Accordingly, they filled in part of the moat surrounding the citadel and demolished the upper section of its wall. The original plan was even more ambitious: it was decided to tear down the row of shops stretching from Jaffa Gate to the Temple Mount, but the cost of the project and the amount of compensation that would have had to be paid to the shop owners came to approximately two million French francs (about ninety thousand Turkish pounds), an expense which the Ottoman authorities were not prepared to undertake even in the name of friendship.

During the course of our tour we will refer repeatedly to the story of Kaiser Wilhelm's visit to Jerusalem and his efforts to promote German political as well as religious interests in the Holy Land. During the next hour of our walk we will view a number of buildings which were the result of nineteenth-century struggles, often of an economic or political nature, between the great powers of the day, but which at times evolved into sectarian religious confrontations.

Mamilla project The Ramparts Walk continues in a northwesterly direction. Through the crenels on the parapet we can see the end of Jaffa Road and the new housing complex of the Mamilla project, which until the Six-Day War was right on the border, overshadowed by the city wall. A defensive concrete wall had been raised across the main road to project New Jerusalem's inhabitants from the bullets of Jordanian snipers, but was demolished when Jerusalem was re-united in the Six-Day War, on June 8th, 1967.

After the war, the Government of Israel expropriated the Mamilla Quarter. Dwellings and shops were emptied and their residents or owners compensated. The well-known architect

17

Porte de Jaffa.

Jaffa Gate — a century ago and today

18

Moshe Safdie was commissioned to plan the reconstruction of the area. The general concept of his plan was the total destruction of all existing buildings, with the exception of the extensive French monastery of St. Vincent de Paul, and the erection of a grandiose complex with a system of underground streets and parking facilities and a huge, modern shopping center.

Safdie's plan aroused much controversy and public opposition. The original scheme did not meet with the approval of planning commissions both because of its extent and complexity, and also since it was believed that it could not be implemented in stages. After undergoing many changes over a period of several years, a simpler and much more modest version was finally approved in 1987, and construction got underway in 1991. What is to be constructed is a complex containing an exclusive housing development, hotels and a shopping center. From the walls of Old Jerusalem we can see the apartment houses, characterized by their rounded balconies, of 'David's Village', as it is to be known. When construction is completed, the former frontier between the old and new sections of Jerusalem will become a bridge linking the two.

Breach in the wall, prepared for the visit of Kaiser Wilhelm II

'David's Village', view from the wall. The King David Hotel at the center skyline

The Latin Patriarchate To the right is a particularly interesting view of Jerusalem: the back courtyards of the houses in the Christian Quarter. On the same side, approximately 100 meters further along, we see a tall building which faces south. It can be recognized by the triangular gable above the main entrance; we are looking at its western wing. This is the Jerusalem Latin Patriarchate building, erected during the 1860's, that serves as the seat of the region's Catholic Patriarch.

The Patriarch stands at the head of the local Catholic hierarchy. During the Byzantine period, as the Church establishment was taking shape, the title of

'No Man's Land' in Jaffa Road, dividing Israeli-held Jerusalem from the Old City

Patriarch was conferred on those who led communities of Christians in the most important centers of the Mediterranean region. Jerusalem, too, was decreed a Patriarchate (after Rome, Constantinople, Antioch and Alexandria), not as a center of economic or political importance, but because of its unique status in Christian history and the political qualifications of the heads of the Church in Jerusalem.

This division was more than organizational in nature; it had religious and ideological implications as well. Christian sects, differing one from the other, developed in the various Patriarchates. Rome became the center of Christianity for all the Latin-speaking areas throughout the central and western Mediterranean, claiming hegemony over all Christendom. It was here that the Catholic Church took its final shape. The Patriarchs of Constantinople became the heads of the Greek-Orthodox Eastern Church. While they recognized the primacy of the popes, they refused to accept Rome's absolute supremacy. The Patriarchs of Antioch and Alexandria withdrew for a time from the organiza-

21

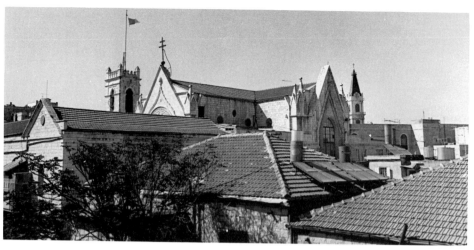

Latin Patriarchate building

tional framework which united Constantinople and Rome. They also attacked Catholic interpretations of the New Testament and were denounced as heretics by the heads of those churches which adopted the appellation 'Orthodox', which means "believers in the true way". In time the Greek and Roman churches drifted further apart until a complete schism came about. For centuries the Patriarchs of Jerusalem were close to the Byzantine Greek Patriarchs in their religious, cultural and organizational outlook. Most were a product of Greek culture and language, except for the period of Crusader rule in Palestine, when the Jerusalem Patriarch was a Catholic.

Under the Mamelukes, leaders of independent Eastern Christian communities in Jerusalem took the title of Patriarch, but the Greek-Orthodox Patriarch retained his senior position. Conflict between the various Christian sects continued throughout the era of Turkish rule, but with the introduction of external powers during the sixteenth and seventeenth centuries, France became the protector of the Latin communities while Russia championed the cause of the Greek-Orthodox communities. The former claimed to uphold Catholic unity while the latter came in the name of the ties between the Greek Orthodox and Russian Pravoslavic churches.

During the lengthy periods in which there was no Catholic Patriarch in the East, Franciscan monks (who first settled in the Holy Land in the early fourteenth century) represented Catholic interests there. They established an order which was granted recognition by the Mameluke rulers and took the title 'Custody of the Holy Land'.

The struggle between the various Christian sects was renewed in all its intensity during the nineteenth century, accompanied by attempts by the European powers to enhance their influence in the Holy Land. The sects vied with each other in establishing schools, building hostels for pilgrims, strengthening their influence among the local population and for outward signs of honor and status. At times the situation degenerated into violence. Increasing intervention by the European powers in ecclesiastical

22

affairs in the Holy Land brought matters to such a point that ostensibly local incidents, such as the disappearance of a silver star from the Church of the Nativity in Bethlehem, developed into international affairs which were part of the causes that led to the outbreak of the Crimean War in 1853.

But as we have already noted, it was not religious devotion alone that led European powers to greater involvement in the region, but political, economic and strategic interests as well, whose importance grew steadily as the condition of the Ottoman Empire deteriorated. The visit to Jerusalem of Kaiser Wilhelm II was no exception to the rule; his concern for ecclesiastical affairs was equalled by that for the economic and political interests of his country.

In 1847, after the establishment of the first Protestant Bishopric in Jerusalem, the Pope appointed a Latin Patriarch for the city. Until then the Franciscan monks had been the only Catholics active among the country's inhabitants; they had instituted an educational system, built pilgrims' hostels and even established a printing press to publish the Scriptures and Church tracts. A Protestant Bishopric had been established in 1841 as a joint venture of Prussian and Anglican clergymen; despite their small number they were highly successful in gathering converts to Protestantism. They apparently preached not only to Moslems and Jews, but to Catholic Arabs as well. Their success led the Pope to found a Latin Patriarchate in the city.

Construction of the Latin Patriarchate building was begun in 1859 and completed five years later. It was built in Italian style: the large building, constructed around an inner courtyard, included a school, a church and a tower.

The Pope's initiative proved to be well-taken. Many Catholic institutions were established throughout the country: hostels, schools, hospitals, churches and monasteries. They were renowned for their high standards, attracting many adherents. Such institutions were set up even in predominantly Greek-Orthodox centers such as Beit Jalla, Jifna, Ramallah and Bir Zeit.

The
icipality
nd City
Plaza

Exactly opposite the northwest corner of the wall you can see a building with a rounded facade —Jerusalem's former City Hall. It was constructed in the early 1930s with funds that Barclay's Bank placed at the disposal of the Jerusalem Municipality, which lacked the necessary financing. In return, the bank received the ground floor, which for many years was its branch in Jerusalem. It's symbol, a double 'B', can still be discerned in the latticework on the windows. Between 1948 and 1967 this building was right on the border of the no-man's land that divided Jordanian and Israeli Jerusalem. The bullet-holes in its walls are silent evidence of the War of Independence in 1948.

The City Plaza, one of Jerusalem's largest and most modern construction projects, was completed in Summer 1993 in the vicinity of the former City Hall. The objective was to concentrate all Jerusalem Municipality offices in one compound surrounding a large City Plaza with an area of about 4,000 sq. meters which will host public performances, ceremonies and mass demonstrations. The area surrounding the Plaza forms an urban complex that integrates restored historic buildings with two modern edifices and three interconnected smaller public squares. Planning of the entire project was done by renowned Canadian architect Jack Diamond in cooperation with three local architectural firms.

French Hospital 'St. Louis' Most of the buildings that we will see on our tour up to the New Gate were established by French Catholic organizations; French influence on their architectural style is evident. Just across the street we see a building constructed by one such Catholic organization—the St. Louis French Hospital. The building can be recognized by its two large wings which reach out to Paratroopers' Street. The building, which has a small garden, serves to this day

St. Louis French hospital

24

as a hospital for chronic diseases and terminal cases and is ope-
rated by the nuns of the Order of St. Joseph.

The St. Louis Hospital was one of the first institutions established by the French outside the Old City walls. It is named after
Louis IX, King of France between 1226-1270, renowned for his
strong religious convictions and his munificent contributions to
the Crusades.

Louis IX led two Crusades in an attempt to wrest the Holy Land from its
Moslem rulers. During the first of them he was taken prisoner by the ruler of
Egypt; the second crusade in which he participated, which began in Tunisia,
cost him his life. Due to his piety, he was canonized by the Church in 1297,
only a few years after his death.

The name of St. Louis is not the hospital's only connection with the Crusades.
During the period of Crusader rule in the Holy Land, a leper hospital named
after St. Lazarus was situated on this site, the remains of which are still
visible between the French Hospital and Notre Dame. The monks who served
in this hospital became the nucleus of a military order that took upon itself to
care for lepers, who until then had been ostracized. During the Middle Ages
lepers were required to wear special garments and to carry a clapper in order
to warn passersby of their horrible, incurable disease.

This twofold connection with the Crusades was not a coincidence. Both the
purchase of the lands upon which the hospital was built and the construction
of the building were the initiative of the Count de Feille, son of a noble family
from the south of France, a devout Catholic and an enthusiastic romantic
whose imagination was fired by the Crusades. He was an amateur artist who
also studied the history and demography of the Middle East. His first visit to
the Holy Land, with his mother, in 1876 at the age of 24, left an indelible
impression upon him. He returned time and again until he made Jerusalem
his main place of residence. He gave freely of his time and resources to
establish Catholic institutions and to acquire various buildings, which had
long ago belonged to the Crusaders, on behalf of these institutions, arranging
and paying for their renovation. He established a number of institutions in
Jerusalem, Nazareth, Abu Ghosh and elsewhere.

De Feille was deeply moved by the idea of building a hospital on the site
where the legendary Crusader leader Tancred camped, and even more so on
the site of the former Crusader leper hospital. Evidence of de Feille's romantic spirit is the fact that he himself decorated the walls of the hospital's
second floor with blazons of the Crusader knights and other paintings illustrating the Crusader period.

During World War I the hospital was commandeered by the Turkish armed
forces who converted it into a military hospital. Although the nuns of the
Order of St. Joseph continued to run the hospital, the Turkish soldiers ruined
its furnishings and even damaged its exterior. They daubed black paint over
de Feille's frescoes. In 1920, an aged and ailing de Feille returned to Jerusalem and restored the paintings of his youth, but he succumbed to cancer in
1924. The devoted nurses of the Order of St. Joseph cared for him tenderly to
his last moment in the very hospital that he had built.

Notre Dame de France   Next to the hospital is the Notre Dame de France Hospice, the crowning glory of French architecture in Jerusalem. The building was erected in order to provide accommodation for the many French pilgrims visiting Jerusalem at the end of the nineteenth century.

The Catholics had first built a hostel inside the city wall; when this accommodation was fully occupied, they set up tents on the plot of land where the hospice was later built. This encampment was under the supervision of a French colonel who lived nearby. In time, the tents could no longer meet the needs of the pilgrims, nor were they in keeping with the standards of their French patrons. Hence the construction of the hospice lasted twenty years, from 1884 to 1904. By the time of its completion, the French monopoly over the interests of Catholics in the Orient had come to an end. The continuous conflict between France and Germany in Europe spurred the Germans to do all in their power

Notre Dame de France in 1948 — war damage is evident

26

Notre Dame de France in 1988

to obtain direct control over German Catholic affairs in the Middle East. The friendly relations maintained by the German emperors with the Ottoman authorities helped them achieve this goal; the visit of the German Kaiser Wilhelm II was the final stage in freeing German Catholics in the Holy Land from French domination.

From Israel's War of Independence in 1948 until the Six-Day war in 1967, the cease-fire demarcation line between Israel and Jordan ran at the foot of this building. One of the Israel Defense Forces frontline posts was situated atop Notre Dame. During the War of Independence, on May 23, 1948, the Arab Legion unsuccessfully attempted to break through the Etzioni Brigade's lines and capture the hospice. The Israeli forces, for their part, failed in their attempt to set up a bridgehead in the Jordanian-held section between Notre Dame and the Mount Scopus enclave. In another unsuccessful operation during the night between July 16 and 17, 1948, they failed to expand Israeli control beyond the New Gate. Thus was drawn the border which divided Jerusalem until 1967. The majestic building continued to tower over the area with one of its wings in complete ruin.

In the early 1960's negotiations were carried out between the Hebrew University and Catholic authorities regarding the purchase of Notre Dame with

27

Concrete wall for protection against snipers' bullets, Zahal Square, 1948-1967

Zahal Square today

the aim of turning it into student dormitories. The transaction was completed and part of the sum was even paid, but the Catholic authorities had second thoughts and cancelled the transaction at the very last moment. In light of Israel's delicate relations with the Vatican, the Hebrew University relinquished its legal rights to the property, receiving some compensation. Only a few years later the Six-Day War changed the entire situation. The 410-room Notre Dame Hospice became a bustling, luxurious hotel for Catholic pilgrims visiting Jerusalem.

We take a few steps along the curve in the city wall and look inside the Old City, where we can discern another Catholic institution: the large Franciscan Monastery, and the New Gate.

The Franciscan Monastery From our vantage point at a corner in the wall, we can see the rear entrance to the monastery. The iron gate bears a red double cross—the emblem of the Franciscan Order. This is the largest and most important Franciscan monastery in Israel. It has served Franciscan monks since 1459 when they purchased it from Georgian monks, after having been expelled a few years earlier from their center on Mount Zion. The monastery is the residence of the head of the 'Custody of the Holy Land' who holds responsibility for all Franciscan monasteries throughout the Middle East. As already noted, until the establishment of the Latin Patriarchate this monastery was the center for all Catholics in the Holy Land, and for that matter in the entire Middle East. The monastery contains fourteen workshops, employing Catholics living in Jerusalem, as well as a hospital, a pharmacy, the Catholic Theological Seminary, schools, administrative offices, a library, a printshop and a large hostel abutting the courtyard. In the past there were spacious food stores, a flour mill and a bakery as well. Large water cisterns are still extant; in the past these enabled the monks, as well as the entire Catholic community in Jerusalem, to be self-sufficient in water.

Over the centuries, from the time the Franciscans established themselves in this monastery, they increased their control and presence in many sites holy to Christianity throughout the Holy Land. They founded the Church of St. Lazarus near the Tomb of Lazarus at Bethany (al-Azarieh), the Church of the Visitation in Ein Karem and—at the beginning of the nineteenth century—the Chapel of the Flagellation on the Via Dolorosa. However, they lost control over other sites, such as the Tomb of Mary and certain sections in the Church of the Nativity. Although the establishment of the Latin Patriarchate in Jerusalem led to enhancement of Catholic activity there and throughout the country, the heads of the Franciscan Order considered this to be an infringement upon their status and fiercely opposed it.

From its establishment, the Franciscan Order has been closely linked with

29

Franciscan Monastery and its steeple

the history of the Holy Land and especially with that of Jerusalem. Its founder, St. Francis of Assisi, visited the Holy Land during the Fifth Crusade. After the expulsion of Crusaders from the country, the Franciscans were the first Christians to reestablish a Catholic monastery. With the permission of the Mameluke rulers, they settled on Mount Zion where they began to construct their first monastery between 1335 and 1337. In addition, they were given control over a number of sites holy to Christianity, such as the Cenacle (the Room of the Last Supper). Eventually, they were also allowed to conduct services in the Church of the Holy Sepulcher. Their privileges increased with time and served as a basis for the establishment of the 'Custody of the Holy Land'. The Order extended its control to include the Church of St. Mary in the Valley of Jehoshaphat and the Church of the Nativity in Bethlehem. Until the nineteenth century, the Franciscan Order was the only Catholic body permanently resident in Jerusalem; the Franciscan monks attended to all matters concerning the large number of pilgrims visiting the Holy City. The Franciscan community was afforded diplomatic protection and economic patronage by the Pope and by Europe's Catholic countries.

During the fifteenth century, a dispute broke out between the Franciscan Order at the monastery and the Jewish community resident on Mount Zion. Documents from the period indicate that the Jews endeavored to oust the Franciscan monks from David's Tomb, in order to establish a place of prayer there for themselves. The upshot was that the Tomb was turned over to the Moslems. Franciscans were at first allowed to pray there, but not for long. In the mid-fifteenth century the area was sequestered by the Moslems, some of the buildings erected by the Franciscans were destroyed and the monks were forced to find other accommodation. Thus, on the site of the Georgian Monastery that they had purchased, the Franciscans erected the St. Savior Monastery which we are now viewing.

The 'New Gate'

Leaving the bend in the wall, we continue along the ramparts and walk above the 'New Gate', where we find the first stairway leading down to the street. From here it is but a short walk to various sites in the Christian Quarter, the church in the Franciscan Monastery and other Catholic institutions. The Church of the Holy Sepulcher is also nearby.

The New Gate is so called because it was the last gate cut in the city wall — in 1889. At the request of the French ambassador in Constantinople, Sultan Abdul Hamid granted permission to breach the walls at this spot in order to facilitate contact between the monasteries within the Old City and the hostels for pilgrims outside the city wall. Hence this gate's Arabic name is 'Bab Abdul Hamid' — the 'Gate of Abdul Hamid'.

From this point until the Damascus Gate, the wall is built on a gradual incline. It curves slightly and then runs close by one of the buildings of the Franciscan St. Savior Monastery (it can be easily identified by the chimney to the north). An iron stairway (not in use) leads from the wall to a pretty garden.

From here, too, we may view the Old City's topography. The wall is built on the slope of the city's northwestern hill, the location of the Christian Quarter. Opposite, to the east, is the hill of Antonia, or Beit Zayta, densely filled with the houses of the Moslem Quarter. The valley running between two hills, i.e. between the Christian and Moslem Quarters, is the main axis of the Old

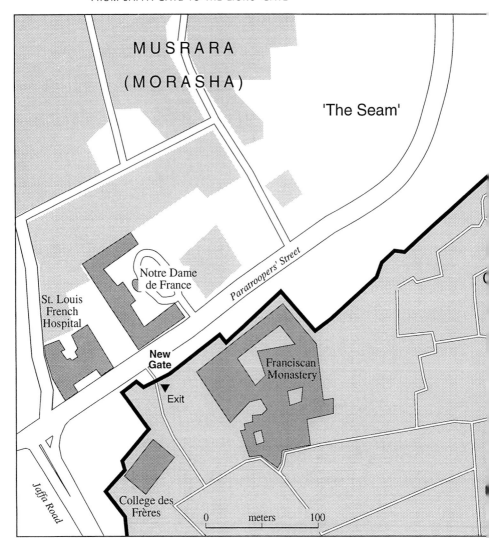

Map 2: From the New Gate to Damascus Gate

City. This is difficult to discern when walking through the alleys, but from our vantage point it is most obvious. This is the dry bed of a stream known by its Greek name, the 'Tyropoeon Valley'. It perhaps may be identified with 'the Valley' referred to in the Book of Nehemiah, so named because of the outstanding role it played in the topography of Jerusalem throughout the ages. The entire Old City of Jerusalem is in fact built on the drainage basin of this riverbed.

32

The New Gate

'Seam' As we walk atop the wall from the New Gate to Damascus Gate
we are presented with an opportunity to look at the empty field
between the Notre Dame Hospice and the houses to the east of
the Street of the Prophets. This area is called 'the seam', because
it is where the mainly Arab-populated eastern section of the city
meets western Jerusalem, which is predominantly Jewish.

From 1948 until the Six-Day War in 1967, this empty area was a no-man's

33

The 'Seam' — No Man's Land in Musrarra prior to June 1967

The 'Seam' in 1994 — Section of Throughway No. 1

land between the eastern city, under Jordanian rule, and the Israeli, western section of Jerusalem. As already noted, the demarcation line ran beneath the walls of the Notre Dame Hospice. Both sides were forbidden by the terms of the Israel-Jordan Armistice Agreement signed in 1949 to build in this area. Even though a relatively long period has passed since the reunification of the city in 1967, there has been no construction on these empty lots. Recently, plans have been drawn up to construct a central square and hotels. If these plans are executed, the former no-man's land will become an area that will contribute to greater unification of Jerusalem's two parts.

Through-vay No. 1 An additional project making fast progress is Throughway no. 1 which will cut through Jerusalem from the French Hill in the North to Bethlehem in the South. The section from the French Hill to Damascus Gate has already been completed; the planned continuation will connect this section with present-day Hebron Road. It is part of a planned highway system for Jerusalem's metropolitan area which is intended to solve the difficult transportation

Domes of the Church of the Holy Sepulcher

35

Facade of the Church of the Holy Sepulcher before renovation, 1870

problems of one of the world's most ancient cities as it faces the twenty-first century.

The Church of the Holy Sepulcher, where Jesus was buried, stands out clearly inside the Old City. Its two gabled domes can be seen to the south, just above the horizon. From here, too, we catch our first glimpse of the golden dome of the Dome of the

Rock (the Mosque of Omar) and the neighboring lead-covered dome of al-Aqsa Mosque, both on the Temple Mount. These are Islam's most holy sites in Jerusalem, and are counted amongst the three most holy places for Moslems in the entire world (Mecca and Medina precede Jerusalem in sanctity).

From our vantage point we can also discern some of Jerusalem's minarets and bell towers. Two of them stand close to the Church of the Holy Sepulcher; others are on the Temple Mount or in other parts of the Moslem Quarter. Most of the church bell towers were raised during the nineteenth or at the beginning of the twentieth centuries. Prior to that, Christians were forbidden by the Moslem authorities to build bell towers above their churches. Furthermore, such towers are architectural appurtenances characteristic mainly of Western European churches, which up to the middle of the nineteenth century constituted a minority among the city's Christian sects. The Eastern churches, which account for the majority of Jerusalem's Christians, did not summon their faithful to prayer by the ringing bells but rather by knocking on a wooden board called *Nakus*.

From atop the minarets that we can see from the wall, the *muezzin* calls the Moslem faithful to prayer (today the voices are recorded and broadcast over loudspeakers). Minarets frequently provide silent evidence of historical disputes between different communities in the city. At times they are constructed in an eye-catching, magnificent style to emphasize the generous contribution of its donor to Islam. The minaret closest to us is Khanqat al-Salihiyya, a fourteenth-century structure built above a Moslem prayer house originally built by Saladin after he captured Jerusalem from the Crusaders in 1187. This Moslem edifice was erected within the confines of Crusader Jerusalem's Latin Patriarchate building, an act graphically illustrating the city's age-old interreligious conflicts.

Damascus Gate As we continue towards Damascus Gate, take careful note of its location. It is situated on the lower slope of the Tyropoeon Valley, which we have already mentioned. This is not surprising, because a city's gate is usually built on the location most convenient to the city's residents and visitors, to be used mainly in times of peace. The valley leading up to it from the north has served since Herodian times as the main approach for travellers coming both from Nablus and from the coastal plain, for even the

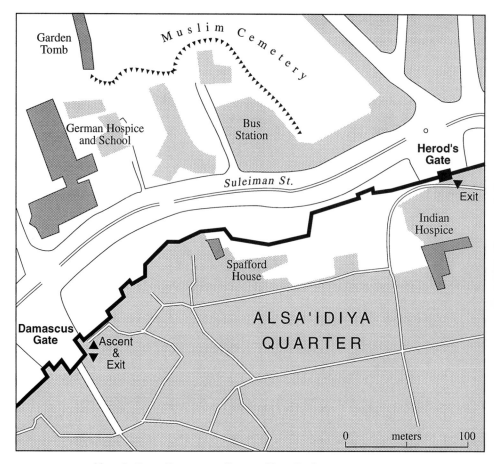

Map 3: From Damascus Gate to Herod's Gate

ancient road from the coastal plain terminated on this side of the city.

The gate's Hebrew name, Shechem (Nablus) Gate, like its ancient Arabic and Latin ones, are evidence of the destination of the road that began here. One name used by Westerners — Damascus Gate — points to the fact that from here one set out northwards to Damascus. The Arabic appellation, 'Gate of the Column' (Bab al-Amud), refers to the gate's former status as the main entrance to the city: a Roman column stood in the gate's square, probably bearing a decorative statue of the Roman emperor.

No remains of this column have been found, but there is evidence of its existence in a sixth-century church discovered at Madaba in Jordan. The mosaic floor of this church included a map of the Holy Land as it was known to the artist who laid it. Parts of the mosaic were destroyed, including impor-

Damascus Gate

tant sections of the map, but luckily most of the map of Jerusalem remained intact, enabling us to learn the layout of Jerusalem at the end of the Byzantine era. (See color pages) The map clearly shows the Roman column, standing inside the city wall in the center of the market place, the layout of Jerusalem's streets and many public buildings.

Damascus Gate, like the other gates of Jerusalem, is known by still another name, associated with Christian tradition. In Crusader times it was called 'St. Stephen's Gate', named for the first Christian martyr, since it led to the spot where his bones were laid to rest as early as the fifth century. In the Middle Ages, Jewish pilgrims called it 'Abraham's Gate'.

We descend to the observation platform looking southwards over the city to get a view of the city's street grid pattern. The square facing the Damascus Gate, a sort of elongated plaza, serves those who enter the city from the north. It is paved with colored stones set in geometric designs. As in the past, this square is today a bustling center of all types of commerce, the location for fairs, and seasonal markets and assemblies held on holidays and festivals. And, of course, it is a place where idlers congregate. Such continuity over the centuries is not surprising.

If we compare the structure of the Old City today with that depicted on the Madaba map, we soon realize that the Roman-Byzantine city plan was so well-designed that its main lines hold true today. The map depicts the Byzantine gate square and the course of the two main roads leading from the square. This indicates that Byzantine Jerusalem was built according to the

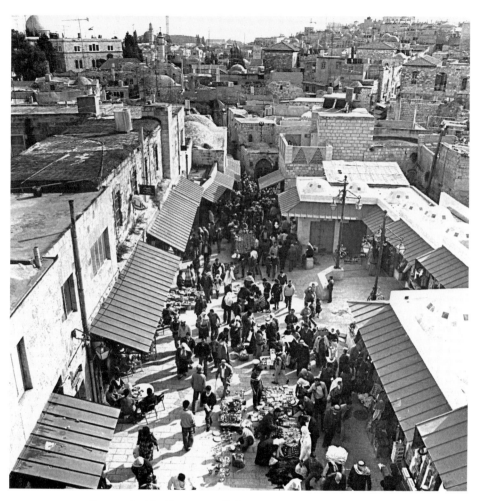

Square inside Damascus Gate

traditional Roman plan, 'the Hippodamian pattern', based upon a network of roads intertwining to form a criss-cross pattern. Wherever possible the Romans built their cities according to this principle. The main north-south street was called the Cardo, while the main east-west artery was known as the Decumanus.

From our observation platform we can see that the Roman plan is still evident. Two streets extend from the southern limits of the square: to the right, the most westward one, Rehov Beit Habad (Olive Press Street), or Suk Khan al-Zayit in Arabic. This is the main commercial street of Jerusalem's Old City, running in a straight line from north to south, despite the unfavorable topography along its course, forcing it to cross two hills and a valley. The left-hand street, the easterly one, the Street of the Valley (Rehov Ha-Gai in Hebrew, al-Wad in Arabic) also preserves the course of the original Roman-Byzantine street. The street is laid along a favorable topographical route, the Tyropoeon Valley. It runs arrow-straight with only one gentle angle, near the junction

40

with the Via Dolorosa, to show that it was laid along the route of the valley. It does not run parallel to other streets, nor does it intersect them; however, even here we have evidence of the Roman penchant for order and planning, quite unlike the manner in which later Old City streets were laid out, with their recurring twists and turns.

Now that we have taken in the landscape seen from the observation platform above Damascus Gate, we can continue our tour. There are three possibilities:

(a) To continue along the ramparts above Herod's Gate to the Lions' Gate (see p. 44);

(b) To leave the Ramparts Walk and take a walking tour through the streets and lanes of the Old City. To do this we must descend from the wall, through a revolving gate to the north of the observation platform, into Damascus Gate Square;

(c) To first visit the ancient sections of Damascus Gate (our recommended choice) and then decide later whether to continue our tour or to stop for a short rest.

If we have decided upon the third option, we descend a few steps from the observation platform to the lower level and from there through a narrow passage to a steep stairway, uncovered in 1979 together with the tower adjacent to the ancient Roman gate, to which it leads.

The eastern tower, which served as the 'guard house', rose to great heights. Almost twelve meters of the original building remain. Only the roof was destroyed so that the Roman tower and gate are one of the most intact remains to survive from Roman times.

Inside the hall is a small exhibit dealing with the Bar Kochba revolt, the Jewish rebellion against Rome following which Hadrian built the pagan city of Aelia Capitolina on the ruins of Jewish Jerusalem after quelling the revolt in 135 CE. Along the northern wall of the hall is a reconstruction of the Roman gate, and next to it is a section of the Madaba map from which we can see the later shape of the gate during the Byzantine period. The Roman Empire was then at the height of its power; the very presence of Roman legions was a sufficient deterrent to guarantee the security of the inhabitants of the Empire's territories. Even though Jerusalem was built as an unwalled city, the Romans constructed an impressive gate at the main approach to the city from the north.

The Roman gate, like others of this period, had three entrances. The central section, the widest and highest, was almost double the size of those that flanked it. The present-day Ottoman gate is built directly above it. The eastern entrance, the one to the left when you face the gate from outside the walls, has remained almost intact and was uncovered in archeological excavations, while the western section of the triple gate is still buried underground. Unlike

41

The Roman gate below Damascus Gate

other gates of the period, two turrets were built, one on either side of the gate.

During a later period the gate area served as an oil press. The archeologists who excavated the site have restored some of the implements used for pressing olives and extracting the oil found on the site. The illustration in the exhibit shows how they were used.

Through the gate's entrance hall we go out to the plaza on the northern side of damascus Gate from where we can look at the remains of the ancient eastern entrance. Above it was a Roman inscription, damaged in later periods, of which only the lower line

Damascus Gate from inside — note the Roman foundations of the left tower

has survived, written in the shortened forms used at the time: COL. AEL. CAP. D.D.- "Colonia Aelia Capitolina, by decree of the city's commanders."

Returning through Damascus Gate, we enter the internal square excavated in 1982. Though various buildings were erected here in later periods, the original paving has survived. The path leads us between these buildings until we reach an elongated hall, about thirty meters long, paved with large stones which have remained on the site since ancient times. Along the walls are illustrations and photographs of the square and restorations of the gate area in various periods of its history.

Square outside Damascus Gate

We return to the roof above Damascus Gate by means of the same stairway which we descended earlier. (Those who wish to rest a bit may refresh themselves in the cafe situated in the square just inside the gate, before making the ascent).

Leaving Damascus Gate, we continue along the ramparts, skirting the Moslem Quarter. From here we can get a look at both the Quarter and the new neighborhoods beyond the city wall. Just outside the wall is the plaza at the entrance to Damascus Gate. It was rebuilt in recent years in the form of a Roman theater. Visitors to the plaza can view the wall above the gate, one of the most beautiful sections of the entire city wall.

Two streets run in a northerly direction from this plaza; the western one (to the left) is the Street of the Prophets which connects eastern and western Jerusalem; this street was sealed off from 1948 until June 1967, when the city was divided. The other is Nablus Road; it too served as a border until 1967. At the beginning of the nineteenth century, when Jerusalem began to expand beyond the city walls, the Nablus Road area was one of the first to be built up. However, since the border later ran along here for some nineteen years, the commercial center of the region developed in nearby Salah al-Din Street, which runs parallel to Nablus Road to the east.

The Schmidt German School From our observation point we can see another building which resulted from European involvement in Jerusalem at the end of the last century; the Schmidt German Hospice and School. This enormous building, located to the east (right) of Nablus Road, was built by German Catholics at the beginning of the twentieth century. As already noted, German involvement in Jerusalem reached its peak with the 1898 visit of Kaiser Wilhelm II.

German Catholics, who have been present in Jerusalem since the 1830's, aspired to a greater presence in Jerusalem than that augured by the cornerstone-laying ceremony for the Catholic Church on Mount Zion. Towards the end of the century they built a hostel and a school on the slope of what is now Hillel Street in the New City. But these institutions were a bit too far away from the Old City, and eventually were unable to provide for the needs of the Jerusalem German Catholic community. The impressive spate of buildings erected by French Catholics also spurred the Germans, highly motivated by nationalist aspirations, to establish additional institutions of their own which would compete with the beautiful French edifices.

In 1899, German Catholics purchased a plot of land for a new hospice. This site held many advantages: although very near the Old City it was outside the walls, beyond the stifling atmosphere inside them. It was centrally located very near Damascus Gate, only a short walking distance from the holy places. Much construction was already underway in this area. The French Dominicans were busy constructing their basilica, and the Anglicans were also engaged in building a complex not far from there. A further, most important consideration in selecting this site was its location opposite Notre Dame, the bastion and pride of the French Catholics. Hundreds of German pilgrims who came in 1898 for the cornerstone-laying ceremony stayed in the Notre Dame Hospice for the lack of a German hostel that could accommodate them.

The Germans were prepared to pay well for a plot of land so suitably located. They even turned to an architect who was their countryman, Heinrich Renard, who planned other buildings erected in Jerusalem at the time. He drew up an ambitious plan for a grandiose building with two wings to face west, in the direction of the Notre Dame Hospice. As it turned out, only part of the plan — the southern wing — was implemented, because the full project was beyond the financial capabilities of German Catholics. The new building included a school for boys, a teachers' seminary, a hospice for Catholic pilgrims, a chapel and a museum. The principal of the school was the German Catholic priest Father Schmidt, after whom it was later named, and the hospice was named for St. Paul. In 1908, Father Ernst Schmitz joined the staff and established a seminary to train teachers to work in the Order's Galilee schools. He brought with him a collection of stuffed animals, trees, minerals, butterflies, snakes, etc. This collection, designed for instructing teacher trainees, was constantly enlarged by Schmitz, who paid large sums for animal carcasses he bought from villagers throughout the country. The

Schmidt German Hospice and School

collection was rediscovered recently and is an important source of informa-
tion about indigenous but since extinct animals. From Summer 1994, the
collection is on display at the new Jerusalem zoo in southwest Jerusalem.
During World War I, the school served as headquarters of German General
Kress von Kressenstein and later housed offices of the British Mandatory
authorities. From the point of view of style and quality of construction, this
building is one of the most outstanding of its kind in Jerusalem: it is a
synthesis of styles and used materials of excellent qualities. An interesting
feature of the building's architecture reflects living conditions at the time of
its construction: a beautiful polygon tower abuts from the southern wall of
the St. Paul Hospice and is connected to the main building at every floor. This
carefully-planned tower houses the lavatories of each floor.

**The
merican
Colony;
pafford
House**

European settlement in Jerusalem at the end of the last century
was not only at the initiative of governments and powerful religious organizations. In a building inside the walls of the Old City,
beyond the point from which we have been observing the German Hospice, an important attempt at settlement was made by a
group of Americans.

This effort was the result of the personal tragedy suffered by the
Spafford family who set out from Chicago in 1873 bound for a
vacation in France. Their ship sank and the four Spafford girls
were drowned. The mother, Anna Spafford, lost consciousness;
when she recovered, she vowed that her life would be devoted to
the service of God and to helping others. When tragedy struck the
Spafford family once more and their baby boy, born after the girls'
demise, also passed away, the Spaffords, together with other
members of their Presbyterian congregation, decided to go to
Jerusalem and seek consolation from their distress in the Holy
City.
   This group arrived in Jerusalem in 1881 and soon thereafter
rented the house in the Alsa'idiya neighborhood which we see
before us. The American group, which at first lived the life of most
Christian pilgrims, soon made friends with both their Arab and
Jewish neighbors. Theirs was a commune and when, in the
course of time, leadership passed to Anna Spafford, a group of
devout Swedish Christians joined them. Together, the two groups
bought a plot of land in the Sheikh Jarrah Quarter (north of the
Old City), where they established a settlement called the 'Swedish Colony' or the 'American Colony'. Over the years it became
quite an attractive neighborhood, now known only as 'The American Colony'. The major building is the attractive American Colony
Hotel.

47

They soon made themselves felt in late nineteenth-century Jerusalem. They founded a school which attracted the children of some of the most influential Moslem families, established a large bakery and developed a photographic service which documented events in the Jerusalem from 1898, the year of Kaiser Wilhelm II's visit, through the first half of the twentieth century. They ran a souvenir shop whose specialty was greeting cards decorated with dried flowers. The income from these cards was devoted to helping the needy. Well-known Swedish author Selma Lagerlof visited the settlers and wrote a moving account of life in this small colony in Jerusalem.

We continue along the wall and soon reach its highest point, from which we look down at East Jerusalem's commercial section, outside the city wall. To the west of the German Hospice is a large commercial edifice with adorned arches on the ground floor section. Behind it is the East Jerusalem central bus station, which has recently undergone extensive renovation. At this point, the wall rises high above all its surroundings.

King Solomon's Quarry On the far side of the central bus station we see a hill with a fenced-off shallow cave. The comparatively low area at the foot of the city wall was formed many years ago as a result of quarrying carried out here to supply stones to build the wall and for the stone buildings within the Old City. Immediately below us is a deep grotto which runs into the bedrock at the base of the wall, though from our position upon the ramparts the entrance to the cave is not visible. Known to the Jews as Zedekiah's Cave, it too is part of the ancient quarries of Jerusalem. 225 meters long, its dimensions impress all who enter it. An ancient tradition identifies this ancient quarry with the story of King Zedekiah's flight from Jerusalem in the face of the advancing forces of Nebuchadnezzar, King of Babylon. According to this legend, the cave begins at this spot in Jerusalem and extends all the way down to the plains of Jericho.

However, this grotto is but a small section of the ancient quarries of Jerusalem. The entire area on which the central bus station is situated, the main road and the adjoining commercial buildings are all part of the quarry area. Later, this area served as a moat for the defense of the city's northern approach, which lacks natural obstacles for its defense. The hills opposite us, on

48

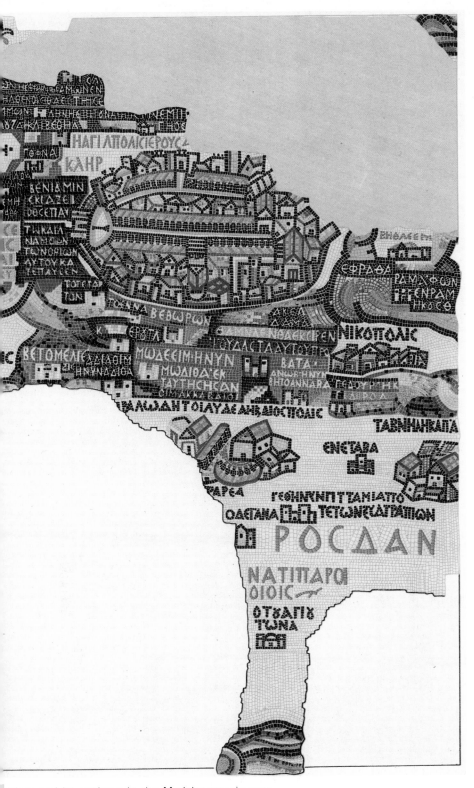

salem and its environs in the Madaba mosaic map

The Citadel by night

ate to the excavations,
ider the southern Turkish wall

Bronze statuette of a cavalryman,
from the Temple Mount Excavations

ial photograph of the Temple Mount and excavations

Model of Jerusalem in the First Temple period, at Rachel Yanait Youth Center
of Yad Izhak Ben-Zvi in the Jewish Quarter

the far side of the bus station and the adjoining buildings, were once part of a plain that ran north of the city; the present 'cliff' was formed by the extensive quarrying activity in the area.

Hill of the Garden Tomb' The left-hand (western) side of the hill is known as 'The Hill of the Garden Tomb'. Here in the 1860's a burial cave was discovered. Swiss scholar Conrad Schick, who discovered the cave, concluded that it was quarried in the Second Temple period. Modern experts in ancient burial customs believe that it can be dated much earlier, perhaps to the First Temple period. The news of the discovery of the burial cave spread quickly, however, and fired the imagination of British general Charles Gordon ('Gordon of Khartoum'), who visited Jerusalem in 1883 and identified the site as the burial place of Jesus.

Gordon, a great soldier and fine administrator, was an adventurer who left his mark on almost every theater of war where the British fought during the nineteenth century. He campaigned in the Crimea, India, China and in the Sudan. Despite his resolute character and military practicality, he was also a romantic. He read the Bible meticulously, seeking answers to mystical issues which were of concern to him. In Jerusalem he set out to locate the exact site of Jesus' crucifixion, and believed that he had found it on the hill opposite Damascus Gate. A short while prior to his visit a burial cave had been discovered on that site, at the time identified as dating from the Second Temple period. To Gordon, the hill had the appearance of a human skull; he believed this to be the origin of the name 'Golgotha' (the skull), the hill upon which the crucifixion took place. To this day many Christians accept Gordon's claim that this is the "true site of the crucifixion"; accordingly many pilgrims daily visit the site reverently. An impressive, beautiful garden has been planted around the cave and is well worth a visit.

The other side of the cliff also took on religious significance during the course of history. It is more difficult to see from where we are standing since it is hidden behind a building which serves today as a branch of the Israel Discount Bank. This building and those contiguous with it are constructed in a half moon shape around the hill on which the al-Sahira cemetery is laid out, one of the two Moslem cemeteries that we will view on our tour.

The hill contains a Moslem cemetery dating from the late Middle Ages. Its name is connected with a passage from the Koran describing the resurrection of the dead at the end of days: "Behold they are coming to Elsahira" (Sura 79:14). The source of the name is not clear. A Moslem legend dating from the early Middle Ages related that all men will gather on the Day of Judgment upon the western slopes of the Mount of Olives. But during

49

the late Middle Ages the tradition changed and the site of the resurrection was identified with the hill we see from here, which was accordingly named Elsahira, as in the quotation from the Koran. During the month of Ramadan, Moslems customarily announce the end of fasting and the beginning of the evening prayer from this site.

Herod's Gate (The Gate of Flowers) We continue on our way and reach Herod's Gate, known in Arabic as 'The Gate of Flowers'. Herod's Gate, like the other gates of Jerusalem, is built along a relatively favorable topographical route, to the west of a small dry riverbed which runs towards the city wall from the north. This valley, today called Beit Zayta, is a tribulet of the Kidron Valley. The Moslem Quarter and the other sections of northeast Jerusalem are built in the drainage basin of this valley.

The name 'Herod's Gate' was given in the late Middle Ages when it was believed that a Crusader church located in the heart of the Moslem Quarter was in fact the remains of Herod's palace. The church was later converted into a mosque called Dayr al-Adas. The Arabic name, 'Gate of the Flowers', is a corruption of Elsahira, the name of the adjacent cemetery (the equivalent of the Arabic letter 'z' replacing the equivalent of the letter 's', thus creating the name Elzahira, 'Flowers'). The gate was kept closed until 1875; its opening heralded the beginning of the Old City's development and its expansion beyond the city walls. When the gate was opened, the first Arab buildings went up outside the walls, many of them spacious private dwellings on large plots of land. In time, the section opposite the gate developed into an Arab neighborhood known as the 'Bab Elzahira Quarter'. During recent renovations of the gate, the original postern has been reopened to visitors.

Rockefeller Museum From atop the gate one is afforded a good view of the area. Beyond the city walls a large white octagonal building stands out on the hill opposite the northeastern corner of the city wall. This is the Palestine Archaeological Museum, generally known as 'The Rockefeller Museum'.

The Rockefeller Museum was opened to the public in January 1938, after eleven years of construction and preparation. Its very construction was made possible almost by chance. In 1925, American millionaire John D. Rockefeller Jr. expressed his wish to donate a large sum of money to establish a museum and research center in Cairo. When this plan did not materialize,

50

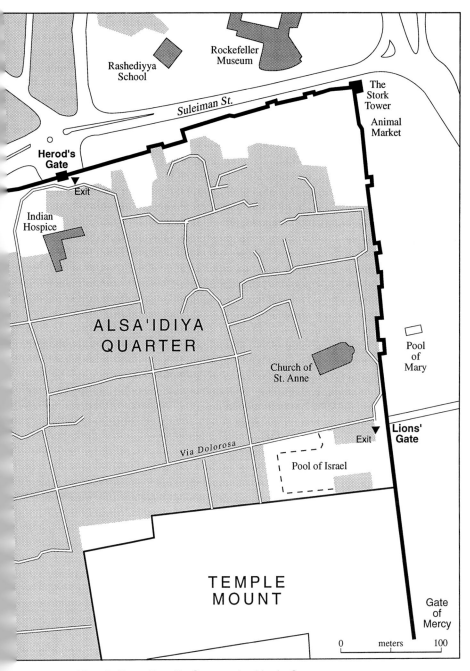

Map 4: From Herod's Gate to the Lion's Gate

Herod's Gate, also know as 'The Gate of Flowers'

James Breasted, One of the leading experts on ancient Egypt and Palestine, who had initiated the original donation for a museum in Cairo, asked Rockefeller to donate part of that sum for the establishment of a museum devoted to the antiquities of Palestine. Rockefeller agreed and in 1927 donated two million dollars for that purpose. The British Mandatory authorities, for their part, set aside a plot of 10 acres for the building, relocating the city abattoir to make this possible.

The building was planned by British architect Austin Harrison, who also designed Government House and the General Post Office building on Jaffa Road. Harrison's plan stressed the features characteristic of architecture in

ew from atop Herod's Gate

ckefeller Museum

Palestine, combining Moslem, Christian and Jewish elements. The octagonal building has been designed to look from the outside like a fortress, fitting in perfectly with the ancient city walls opposite. The interior contains many oriental architectural elements such as domes, vaults, latticework and Armenian ceramic tiles, all of the highest quality and characteristic of the designers' attention to detail. Even a special quarry was opened, on Jericho Road, to provide stone for the building. Artist Erich Gil was invited to Jerusalem to create stone reliefs and a stone fountain for the exhibition plaza. He also designed special lettering in Hebrew, Arabic and Latin for the inscriptions on the walls of the exhibition halls which would follow the style of the lettering found in ancient inscriptions in Palestine.

The Museum also housed the offices and storerooms of the Mandatory Government Department of Antiquities. When the British Mandate came to an end an international Board of Governors was established to ensure the continued administation of the museum and its holdilngs. A world-renowned archeologist, the late Professor E.L. Sukenik, was appointed to the Board as representative of the Hebrew University, but was to all effects prevented from fulfilling any function as the museum was located after 1948 in Jordanian-controlled territory. The Jordanian Government nationalized the museum on October 2, 1966, only eight months prior to the Six-Day War, and thus it automatically reverted after June 1967 to the Government of Israel together with all Jordanian Government property in the eastern section of Jerusalem. During that war, a fierce battle raged around the museum until the site was captured by Israeli troops.

The Rockefeller Museum is now an integral part of the Israel Museum, mounting temporary exhibitions in addition to permanent displays of its extensive collection of Palestine antiquities which were unearthed in excavations throughout the country until 1948. These include prehistoric remains such as relics of ancient man found in the Carmel caves as well as findings from digs in Jericho, Megiddo, Lakhish, Beit Shean, and other sites, including a wide range of ancient statuettes and exquisite ornaments. The building also houses the offices of the Israel Antiquities Authority and the museum's extensive archeological library which serves researchers and scholars. The grounds surrounding the buildings are beautifully landscaped, and are outstanding for their flowers and ancient olive trees.

We now turn back to sites within the Old City which can be seen from above Herod's Gate. We can discern a street leading south to a one-storeyed building bearing the insignia UNICEF. This building once served as a hostel for Moslem pilgrims and religious functionaries from India, hence its name 'Prayer Chamber of the Indians'.

The Northern Moat From the top of Herod's Gate we continue in an easterly direction to the northeastern corner of the city wall. The wall here does not follow a clear topographical course: it crosses a ridge (upon which the Rockefeller Museum stands) and a shallow ravine (where the Rashediyya Arab high school is located). Nor is there any topographical obstacle, such as a moat, running parallel to the wall, or any natural slope which would help to defend this side of the city. Here, the security of Jerusalem's inhabitants is dependent solely on man-made fortifications such as the city wall and the moat on the outside. For this reason, there were periods when Jerusalem's attackers, seeking to exploit this shortcoming, endeavored to enter the city from its northern, less-defended side. Those who erected Jerusalem's walls throughout the ages did their utmost to overcome this deficiency by strengthening the northern fortifications and deepening the moat north of the wall. Like similar moats defending fortresses and citadels throughout the country, it had a dual purpose: to prevent the enemy from bringing up its artillery close to the wall and to forestall any attempt to breach or scale it.

The walls of the moat effectively added to the height of the city wall, thus increasing its defenders' sense of security.

Many conquerors have attacked Jerusalem from the north. On two occasions Roman armies succeeded in taking the city from the north. This was done the first time in 63 BCE by Pompey's legions. The second occasion was when the Jewish Revolt against Rome was quelled in 70 CE. We have no evidence of the city wall's exact course during the Second Temple period, nor do we know exactly how it was defended. However, there are reliable descriptions of the course of the wall in later periods, from which we learn that at least one attack was mounted precisely at this spot. On July 15, 1099, Crusader troops breached the wall immediately opposite the site of present-day Rashediyya school, after a month-long siege during which the Crusaders changed the deployment of their troops a number of times, as well as the sites of their siege weapons. (During the actual conquest, an additional Crusader force sought to breach the city wall at yet another point, on Mount Zion, which also lacked good natural defenses).

The Crusader 'Jewish Quarter' The Crusaders broke through at this point, entering the northwest quarter of the city, which they called the 'Jewish Quarter'. During the period of Crusader rule, Jews no longer inhabited this quarter, only Christians belonging to the eastern sects, but the Crusaders nevertheless persisted in referring to it as the 'Jewish Quarter'. There is some disagreement among scholars as to when Jews resided in this quarter, most probably prior to the Crusader period; the handful of Jews whom the Crusaders allowed to remain in Jerusalem lived in the southwestern section of the city near the Tower of David and probably made a living mainly as cloth dyers.

The section of the city purported to have been the Jewish Quarter in Crusader times is sparsely populated today, giving the impression of having an almost agricultural character. The few widely-scattered houses are separated by tilled plots and vegetable gardens. Not so long ago, at the end of the nineteenth century, many sections of the city looked precisely like this. This would appear to contradict what we know of population density in Jerusalem at the end of the last century and the commonly-accepted image of a Mediterranean Moslem city. For even here and now, in the center of the Moslem Quarter of Jerusalem, are vacant lots used to raise home-grown vegetables. This is one more unique facet of Jerusalem—and of other cities in the hilly areas of Israel—the existence of agricultural plots in the heart of populated areas. The fact that Jerusalem is surrounded by a wall and that it has been densely populated for many generations only makes this phenomenon even more interesting.

The northeastern corner of the city wall contains what is popularly known as 'The Stork Tower'. The origin of the name is unclear, but this massive tower has been so termed since Mameluke times.

Mount Scopus The top of the tower offers a view of the slopes and summit of Mount Scopus. The Hebrew University campus buildings immediately meet the eye. Most of them were erected following the Six-Day War around the original nucleus of buildings built on the summit for the universtiy after World War I.

From Mount Scopus one can observe Jerusalem and its environs. 'Scopus' is derived from the Greek translation of the original Hebrew term *Hatsofim,* meaning 'the observers'.

The mount is first mentioned in Josephus' description of the legendary meeting between Alexander the Great and the High Priest who came out to greet him as he entered Jerusalem in 332 BCE. In his description of the Roman siege of Jerusalem in 70 CE, Josephus also notes that the Roman legions camped on the slopes of Mount Scopus. The Hebrew name also appears in the Palestinian Talmud: "He who sees Jerusalem from 'Hatsofim' must tear his clothing"—in grief, upon seeing the city in its state of destruction. For centuries Mount Scopus was desolate and foresaken, but at the end of the nineteenth century Sir John Grey Hill, a devout English Christian, bought a plot of land on its summit, built a villa there in which he lived a life of seclusion and observed Beduin life patterns. When the British captured Jerusalem from the Turks in December 1917, their troops bivouacked nearby and a nearby plot was turned into a cemetery for the war dead. After World War I, the cornerstone of the Hebrew University was laid here and the Grey Hill villa became the first of its buildings.

View toward Mount scopus. In the foreground — the Rockefeller Museum; left skyline — the Hebrew University; upper central slope — the Jerusalem Center for Near Eastern Studies; right skyline — Augusta Victoria Hospital

Hebrew University

The origins of the Hebrew University in Jerusalem go back to the late nineteenth century. As early as 1882, Professor Zvi Hermann Shapiro, one of the early members of the 'Hovevei Zion' (Lovers of Zion) organization and an advocate of the revival of the Hebrew language, published a series of articles in the Hebrew newspaper *Hamelitz,* calling for the establishment of a Jewish national university in Jerusalem. Professor Shapiro, who taught at the University of Heidelberg, was probably influenced by the nationalist sentiments popular at that time among German intellectuals. The idea of establishing a university also intrigued Theodor Herzl, founder of the modern Zionist movement. He tried to obtain permission from the Ottoman authorities, promising them that the Jewish university in Jerusalem would be open to all other citizens of the Ottoman Empire. Herzl failed, but Chaim Weizmann, an important Zionist leader who later became the first President of Israel, continued to promote the idea, which began to take shape following the British conquest of Jerusalem at the end of 1917. The cornerstone was laid in 1918. Seven years later the University was inaugurated in an impressive ceremony on the summit of Mount Scopus. The participation of Lord Balfour (former British Secretary for Foreign Affairs), General Allenby (commander of the British troops which freed Palestine from Turkish rule), Dr. Chaim Weizmann and

57

Herbert Samuel (first British High Commissioner for Palestine), as well as many scholars and other dignitaries added to the event's significance for Jewish national aspirations. The participants considered the foundation of the university as an important step and it has since achieved a unique status in the renaissance of the Jewish people in its ancestral homeland. This status had been enhanced over the years, as the buildings of the Hadassah University Hospital, the Jewish National and University Library and other institutions were erected on Mount Scopus.

At the end of Israel's War of Independence in 1949, Mount Scopus remained an Israeli-occupied enclave in Jordanian-held territory, cut off from the Jewish section of the city. The resulting cessation of academic activity on the hill only enhanced its symbolic significance for Israelis. The University continued to function in temporary premises scattered throughout west Jerusalem, and the construction of a new campus began in the 1950s at Givat Ram. But the strong emotional tie to the inaccessible national symbol did not wane. When the area was liberated in 1967, the University quickly began a massive campus development program on the mount. Today the expanded facilities house the Faculties of Humanities, Social Sciences and Law. Also here are the new premises of the Bezalel Academy for the Arts, the University administration building and student dormitories. The Hadassah University Hospital buildings have been renovated and are functioning once more.

The Augusta Victoria Hospital To the right of Mount Scopus we can discern a tower with its lower part enclosed in a grove of pine trees. This is the bell tower of the church of the German Hospice 'Augusta Victoria', which rises to a height of 60 meters. One of the last structures to be erected by the Germans in Jerusalem, it was built at the initiative of Kaiser Wilhelm II, who named it for his wife. It originally served as a hospice and recreation home for the German residents of Palestine. Here, as in other buildings, the Germans invested large sums to embellish the building and stress the important German contribution to the development of the city as well as the power of the German Empire.

A well-known architect, Robert Leibnitz, was brought specially from Germany to supervise construction; expert craftsmen were employed to execute the complex decorative motifs. Even the furniture was brought from Germany aboard a special ship. The builders paid particular attention to the construction of the church, which was designed in a style reminiscent of ancient Byzantine churches. It is decorated by magnificent mosaics, with the Kaiser and his wife serving as the dominant characters, as was the custom with rulers in the Byzantine period. Wilhelm intended that visitors gain the impression that the new German Empire was a direct continuation of the glorious days of Frederick Barbarossa and Friederich II, the German emperors who joined the Crusades to the Holy Land. There was also, of course, the influence of competition with the other European powers, a rivalry which is reflected in all of the European construction in Jerusalem in the late nineteenth and early twentieth centuries.

During World War I, Augusta Victoria served as headquarters for the German and Ottoman armed forces in Palestine. When the British forces captured it, they too used it for their headquarters. Later it became the residence of the British High Commissioner. In 1927 it was damaged by an earthquake. Since then, the church — which was hardest hit — is seldom used; even the bell tower, the builders' pride, suffered damage and its height reduced by a few meters. After the earthquake, the High Commissioner moved to newly-built Government House. Augusta Victoria later turned into a hospital, which still functions under the auspices of UNRWA, the United Nations Relief and Work Agency. The church has recently been renovated and is once again open to visitors.

The Jerusalem Center for Near Eastern Studies

On the slope of Mount Scopus facing us, southwest of the Hebrew University, we can see the new building — easily recognizable because of its arches, of the Jerusalem campus of Brigham Young University, called the Jerusalem Center for Near Eastern Studies. It was erected during 1985-1987, not without opposition from some orthodox Jews who feared that it might become a base for missionary activity. The building is today considered one of Jerusalem's most beautiful and impressive edifices, and is open to visitors.

Beneath the Stork Tower, we can see one more site of interest: the monument erected by Arab residents of Jerusalem in memory of Jordanian soldiers who fell during the Six-Day War.

As we continue our tour we will see several cemeteries belonging to various communities: Jews, Moslems, Catholics and Protestants. Burial in the vicinity of the walls of Jerusalem is more than the mere natural requirement of a large city. According to Jewish belief, later adopted by other monotheistic religions, Jerusalem will be the site of the resurrection of the dead in the End of Days. This will occur in the valley between the Mount of Olives and the Temple Mount. All men will stand for final judgment on this site and from there shall come forth redemption. Thus it is considered a great privilege to be buried near the holy places and the site where human suffering will come to an end.

Mount of Olives

Climbing the stairs to the left of the next tower, the one after the Stork Tower we face eastward, towards the Mount of Olives. On its slope is a large Jewish cemetery and atop its summit stands a

The Church of Mary Magdalene, with the Church of Gethsemane in the foreground

tower — the most southerly of the three towers built along the ridge of Mount Scopus and the Mount of Olives. This tower is part of the Russian Orthodox church built during the 1870's and 1880's to mark the site from which Jesus ascended to heaven according to Christian tradition.

Since ancient times, the Mount of Olives has been connected with Jewish traditions of redemption. In the Book of Zechariah it is written: "And his feet shall stand in that day upon the Mount of Olives, which is before Jerusalem on the east, and the Mount of Olives shall cleave in the midst thereof toward the east and toward the west, and there shall be a very great valley; and half of the mountain shall remove toward the north, and half of it toward the south" (14:4). This tradition was maintained even after the country was conquered by the Moslems. Many Jews made pilgrimages to the mount, especially during the Hebrew month of Tishri (September) and for the Hoshanna Rabba festivities at the end of the Feast of the Tabernacles. From here, the spiritual leader of Palestinian Jewry would announce the days on which the Hebrew months would begin, as well as the occurrence of leap years. The Mount of Olives was believed to be the site where the Divine Presence faced the Holy Tabernacle and was thus was most propitious for the conduct of prayers on festivals. It was even referred to as 'the footstool of our Lord'. The fact that the mountain was connected with the tradition of redemption and resurrection of the dead is apparently the source of a Jewish custom, dating to the eleventh century, of burying the dead precisely on this mount. At the beginning of the Byzantine period, Christians identified on the Mount of Olives the locations where Jesus taught his disciples the Lord's Prayer, of his entrance into Jerusalem, where he was delivered into the hands of the Romans and from where he ascended to heaven. The Moslems adopted many of these traditions and added more of their own.

Two Russian churches stand on the Mount of Olives: the Church of the Ascension and the Church of Mary Magdalene (also known as the 'onion-dome church' because of the shape of its cupolas). There are also a number of Roman Catholic churches, the most outstanding being the Church of Gethsemane (the Church of Agony), noted for its embellished facade and the exquisite mosaics at its entrance. There are also a German monastery, two Greek Orthodox monasteries and an additional important church belonging to both the Greeks and Armenians: situated at the bottom of the slope in the Kidron Valley, this is the Tomb of the Virgin, where Mary is believed to have been buried.

Most of these were built on the ruins of ancient churches; they also preserve ancient traditions of sanctity. But despite the mountain's holiness to all Christian communities, only one church—the Church of the Assumption—existed there prior to 1870. In the short period between 1870 and 1894 seven more churches and monasteries were erected, and between 1910 and 1924 three more were built by various communities. The construction of these churches was made possible by generous contributions from European powers of the time.

The Mount of Olives has always been sacred to Jews, so when the Moslems built mosques on the Temple Mount, the Jews moved their main places of prayer to sites in the vicinity of the Temple Mount or to those from which they could easily observe it. Thus, the summit of the Mount of Olives also became a point of pilgrimage for Jews during the first period of Moslem domination.

The slopes of the Mount of Olives were of the utmost significance in regard to burial. In addition to the belief common to Jews, Christians and Moslems that this would be the site of the redemption on the Day of Judgment, there were naive Jews who throughout the ages believed that whoever was buried on the Mount of Olives would be absolved from punishment after death (the blows administered to the body by evil spirits after it has been buried) and spared the necessity of 'the ingathering of souls' (the belief that the bones of the dead would 'roll' to the Mount of Olives, to be miraculously present at the resurrection). At first the Jews buried their dead on the slope below the Temple Mount, but by the fourteenth century they were forced, under pressure from the Mameluke rulers, to move to the opposite slope, i.e., that of the Mount of Olives. The Jewish cemetery on the slope of Mount Moriah now became a place where Moslems buried their dead. In the meantime, the Jewish necropolis expanded to such an extent that at the beginnig of the twentieth century it already covered the major part of the Mount of Olives, especially its western and southern slopes. Jews throughout the world bought burial plots here and many came to Jerusalem in their old age to die and be buried on the Mount of Olives. The Jewish community in Jerusalem often had to defend its claim to the area against those of other minority communities, as, for example, when they successfully prevented the Franciscans from reviving the traditional Passover procession from the top of the Mount of Olives down into Jerusalem.

Lions' Gate We descend the stone steps on the other side of the tower and continue our tour until we see the Church of St. Anne, to our right. This is one of the beautiful Crusader churches in Jerusalem which have survived. A few meters further on, we come to stairs that lead down from the city wall to the street below. We descend by these stairs and continue along the street until we reach the square at the entrance to the Lions' Gate.

The Lions' Gate is the only open gate in the eastern wall of the Old City. It bears many names: the Arabs called it 'The Gate of the Tribes' as well as 'The Gate of Our Lady Mary'; Christians have referred to it as 'The Gate of Jehoshaphat', 'St. Stephen's Gate' and 'The Gate of the Mount of Olives'. 'The Lions' Gate' is its most recent name, having been called thus by Jews since the middle of the nineteenth century. We exit through the gate and observe its eastern facade. On either side are two double reliefs of lion-like images; hence the gate's name. Some believe that

The Lions' Gate

The Ecce Homo Arch in the Via Dolorosa (early twentieth century)

these reliefs were the heraldic emblem of the Mameluke Sultan Baybars who ruled Palestine — and Jerusalem — from 1260. Similar reliefs, bearing the images of panthers, have been found on other buildings known to have been erected by him. A Moslem chronicler who served in Baybars' court describes a khan built by him near the city at the end of the thirteenth century. These reliefs on the gate may well be those that once adorned the entrance to that khan, no sign of which remains. On June 7, 1967, during the Six-Day War, Israeli paratroopers fought their way through the Lions' Gate to capture the Old City, after having previously taken the Mount of Olives.

This brings us to the end of the first part of our tour. South of this point the city wall meets the Temple Mount wall; for security reasons, we are unable to walk through that area. You can reach the city center by taxi or Bus no. 1.

You also have another possibility — to continue afoot. Reenter the Lions' Gate and walk towards the Via Dolorosa, the route of Jesus' agonizing procession bearing the Cross. It is lined with many churches and monasteries, and will lead you to the center of the Old City at the Church of the Holy Sepulcher. From there it is a short walk to Jaffa Gate. This route's advantage is that it gives us a chance to visit the center of the Old City, inside the walls. You can also stop for a snack at one of the area's many small restaurants or coffee bars and perhaps buy some souvenirs.

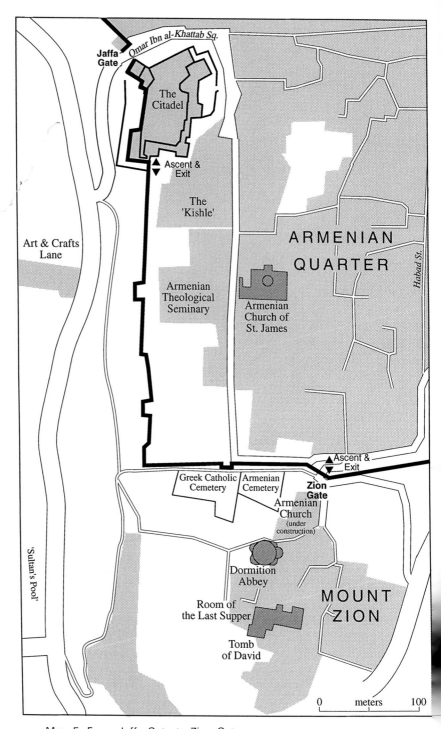

Map 5: From Jaffa Gate to Zion Gate

66

PART TWO

From Jaffa Gate via the Citadel to the Dung Gate

[Buses to Jaffa Gate: 3, 13, 19, 20, 30
Buses from the Dung Gate: 1, 2, 99]

The second part of our tour around the Old City walls starts at the square outside Jaffa Gate. Before ascending the ramparts for a view of the Old City from the west to the south, we suggest a visit to the Jerusalem Citadel, which is now a museum for the history of Jerusalem.

On our way to the Citadel we enter the Old City through the Jaffa Gate into Omar ibn al-Khattab Square, the Moslem Caliph credited with the capture of Jerusalem in 638 CE. To our left is a row of structures erected during the Ottoman period: the tomb of the 'Turkish architects' (see above, p. 14), and an open-sided building which houses the New Imperial Hotel. To our right is the Citadel, its wall defended by a narrow moat. The road veers to the right with a narrow lane branching off to the left — this is David Street, the Old City's main thoroughfare. We stop for a moment in the turn of the road for a view of the Citadel's northeastern tower, literally towering above us. This is the largest and oldest of the Citadel's towers. Beyond the external wall (termed a barbican) built to defend the tower on its outer side, we can see the giant ashlars of the tower's lower tiers. This is its most ancient section, built during the reign of King Herod, about 20 BCE. Herod also erected two additional towers nearby. The three were named after his beloved wife Mariamne, a friend known as Hippicus and his brother Phasael.

'David's Tower' The upper section contains a tower built of smaller stone blocks. This section was constructed about 1200 years after the lower tiers, during the Middle Ages. At first, the tower was much higher than it is today, deeply impressing all who saw it. Even Titus, the Roman general who conquered Jerusalem and

67

Entrance to the Citadel, from the east

Minaret of the Ottoman mosque in the Citadel

quelled the Jewish revolt in 70 CE, ordered that Herod's three towers be preserved so that they "would relate unto the last generation how the great city with its strongly fortified towers was conquered by the courage of the Romans" (Josephus *The Jewish War* 7:1). Titus did not hesitate to destroy most of the city's magnificent structures, including the Temple and Herod's palace. But he relented in the case of these towers, a good example of the art of military defense of that era. Titus' hope, that these towers would recount the strength of Jerusalem's fortifications was at least partly achieved. The vagaries of time have only slightly eroded the bottom section of one of the towers, so that the Second Temple period fortifications continue even today to impress visitors.

During the Byzantine period, Christian monks lived in the tower, to which they referred as the 'Tower of David'; the appellation stuck and is popularly used to this day. Despite the fact that there has never been any connection between King David and the tower, it has been called the 'Tower of David' by various conquerors throughout the generations. Thus, the Moslems gave it the name 'Mihrab Daud', meaning the place where, according to the Koran, King David secluded himself for prayer. Even the Crusaders referred to it as the 'Tower of David'.

The Citadel Steps We walk up the steps to the entrance of the Citadel, which today houses the Jerusalem History Museum. These steps have earned a place in history thanks to the Citadel and the Tower. It was here, on December 11, 1917, that General Allenby, Commander of the British forces which captured Jerusalem during World War I, entered the city. Heading a victory parade, he chose to ascend a platform erected at the top of these steps in order to read out a proclamation from the military authorities. Clergymen representing all the communities present at the ceremony heard, in several languages, that it was the intention of the British conquerors that "every sacred building, monument, holy spot, shrine, traditional site, endowment, pious bequest or customary place of prayer, of whatsoever form of the three religions, will be maintained and protected according to the existing customs and beliefs of those to whose faiths they are sacred." It was no chance decision to hold the moving ceremony at this spot. Throughout the centuries of Mameluke and Ottoman rule, the entrance to the Citadel had come to symbolize the local seat of government. As with the Roman conquest 1850 years previously, the walls fortifying the western section of the city were symbols of its defensive might. So pause a moment on these steps; remember that while they may not be particularly impressive today, they were witness to important and moving historical events.

The Citadel's design was based mainly on plans drawn up by fourteenth-century Mameluke builders, at the time when the city walls lay in ruins and

70

the Citadel was the only fortification able to withstand enemy attacks. Its only approach is across a stone bridge above a moat, which prevented the enemy from moving siege machines close enough to the walls to breach them. Even when the Ottoman Turks rebuilt the city wall, and the Citadel was no longer the only fortification, its moat remained impregnable. Thus the Citadel could be defended not only against enemies attacking from without, but also against attacks from within the city, the survival of its garrison being assured even in the event that the entire city were to fall into enemy hands.

The Citadel's External Courtyard We continue over the reconstructed wooden drawbridge which was raised when the Citadel was under siege. To the left, just before the entrance to the museum, there is a tiny courtyard with a small garden and fountain. Its gate bears a Turkish inscription—one of the few such inscriptions in the entire city—evidence that this courtyard was built in the Ottoman period. It served as an open-air mosque for the Turkish guard garrisoned in the Citadel. Few sections of the Citadel were constructed by the Ottoman Turks, the open-air mosque and stone bridge being notable exceptions. Most of the other sections apparently date from earlier periods, especially during the third decade of the fourteenth century, when Palestine was ruled by Mameluke Sultans whose seat of government was in Cairo.

David's Tower — The Museum We suggest a visit to the Jerusalem History Museum in the Citadel. Visiting hours are Sunday—Thursday from 10 AM to 4 PM, Fridays and Saturdays from 10 AM to 2 PM; there are guided tours in English daily at 11:30 AM. The museum provides visitors with an overview of Jerusalem's history throughout the ages through the use of the most modern mediums. The price of admission includes free access to other parts of the Citadel as well as to the excellent observation point situated on its roof.

The Citadel's gates were laid out at complex angles so as to prevent direct enemy access into the city's main fortifications. They also have other means designed to make its capture difficult: an iron grille to prevent the enemy from destroying the gate behind it; embrasures through which defenders could watch movements near the gate, etc. Inside the entrance hall is an octagonal room with two exits; one, to the right, leads to an observation platform, while the other, to the left, opens on to the courtyard. Let's first climb the winding stairs to the observation platform on the roof, at the base of the Tower of David. There is yet another observation post further up the tower which we will visit later.

71

The observation platform offers a view of the Citadel's courtyard, an excellent vantage point enabling us to grasp the importance of the archeological excavations carried out intermittently on this site from the 1930's through the mid-1980's. The later digs took place at the time that the Citadel was being restored and prepared as a tourist site. Among the important finds at the Citadel are the remains of a wall in the center of the courtyard, first erected in the Second Temple period. Since it was first built, it has undergone changes which apparently made it functional in later periods as well. The wall serves as the base for protruding towers built during the Second Temple period. Of special interest in the excavations within this ancient wall are the base of a circular structure, probably part of medieval fortifications, and a solitary arch straddling remains whose age has not been conclusively established by archeologists.

The most obvious and best-known structure in the Citadel is an elongated conal-shaped minaret, an additional relic from Ottoman Turkish construction efforts. It makes the Citadel stand out even for those who view it from the west, giving its western side

Courtyard of the Citadel

an impressive facade which has captivated the imagination of artists since the beginning of this century. It has appeared in literally hundreds of paintings, stamps and scenic postcards, until it became one of the symbols of Jerusalem. The name 'Tower of David', affixed to many of these illustrations, led to a popular misconception: many believed this minaret to be none other than the 'Tower of David'. Things went so far as to create a popular legend to the effect that King David stood atop this Turkish minaret while watching Bathsheba bathe in the adjacent 'Sultan's Pool'...

Historical records, as well as the conclusions of archeologists, indicate that almost throughout its entire history, this Citadel was fortified and better guarded than any other section of the city. This applies not only to the days of the Second Temple or the years of Mameluke rule, when the present Citadel was built. It would seem that during most of its history, Jerusalem's defenders set up their main fortification close to the city gate which faced west. This was no coincidence; strategic and topographical factors dictated the Citadel's location.

Jaffa Gate stands on a flat portion of land, wedged between the hill on which the Christian Quarter is built and Mount Zion, which today contains the Armenian Quarter. As the city's topography has not changed, there has been no change in the considerations which dictated the gate's location or the construction of the city's main fortifications in this area. Furthermore, Herod's decision to erect on this site the three mighty towers which guarded his palace, together with Titus' choice not to destroy them, were certainly instrumental in the decisions of later builders to construct fortifications on the very same spot. The remains of the original massive structures were used successively as a basis for later construction.

Let us now climb to the highest observation point, on the roof of the Citadel. Special wooded ramps have been added to make it easier to view the surroundings.

The reasons for constructing the Tower of David on this particular site become obvious when the vicinity is viewed from the top of the tower. From here we can see the flat land between the hill on which the Christian Quarter stands (to the north) and Mount Zion (to the south). Further on we see the bell tower of the Franciscan Monastery, whose upper, black section sets it apart from all other towers in Jerusalem.

Slightly to the east, we can see the two domes of the Church of the Holy Sepulcher. Adjacent to it is the white, square bell tower of the Lutheran Church of the Redeemer. As we look more to the east we see the Rockefeller Museum's octagonal tower, the mosques on the Temple Mount, and the houses of the Jewish and the Armenian quarters.

From this vantage point we can also see the Pool of Hezekiah, sometimes known as 'The Pool of the Towers' — completely surrounded by buildings. From this angle it seems to be just in front of the Church of the Holy Sepulcher.

During the Second Temple period, the Pool of Hezekiah was part of the water supply system of Jerusalem. (The connection of this pool with Hezekiah is unfounded, for he ruled at the end of the First Temple period.) Though it has survived until our times, all traces of its pipes have disappeared. During the winter it does hold some water, unfit for human use.

In order to facilitate observation by the garrison, balconies were built on girders straddling the crenels on the ramparts. To increase 'firepower', scaffolding was added around the wall, making it possible for two rows of defenders to use their weapons more effectively. Those standing on the scaffolding could fire at the enemy below without obstructing the aim of the next line of defenders, standing on a lower level, at the same targets outside the Citadel. The sides of the crenels on the wall contain square apertures that apparently held wooden ledges upon which the ammunition and weapons were placed.

Having finished our observation from the roof, we descend the same staircase which we earlier ascended. We now enter the hall to the right, where a short animated film depicting the history of Jerusalem is being shown. Following the red arrows, we start our tour of the permanent exhibition. In each hall a different period in the city's history is depicted, using the most modern techniques. The first hall we enter, in the eastern tower, is devoted to the First Temple period. From there, the red arrows will lead us along a fascinating journey through the ages until twentieth-century Jerusalem.

After completing the chronological tour, it is well worth visiting one of the most interesting exhibits on display in the museum — a model of nineteenth-century Jerusalem. It is on display in an underground room under the western tower, which is actually a restored cistern. This model was built by Stefan Illes, a Hungarian bookbinder, for an international exhibition in Vienna in 1873. After the exhibition closed down, the model was forgotten until rediscovered in Europe a few years ago and brought to Jerusalem through the efforts of a few students at the Hebrew University. It gives us a faithful depiction of Jerusalem and its immediate surroundings in the late 1860s, during a very early stage of construction outside the walls of the Old City.

Upon examination of this model, it may come as a surprise to see how few buildings existed outside the walls of the Old City at that time, for the first houses were built outside the city wall in the 1860's. Note also the flags of the various European nations which maintained consulates, representing their interests in the region. These countries were involved in the massive building projects in the city during the nineteenth century. One very interesting feature in the model is the telegraph line leading into the city from the west. At the time when Illes constructed his model, this was an almost revolutionary innovation in Jerusalem.

In addition to the red route, which led us through the historical exhibits, there are two other routes that can be followed: the blue arrows lead us to observation points atop the walls and towers of the Citadel, while the green arrows will point us to archeological remains that have been unearthed on its premises.

In order to continue the Ramparts Walk, we must exit the Citadel through its western entrance back to the square in front of Jaffa Gate. It was built by the Ottoman Turks during the sixteenth century to serve as an artillery ground.

The Turks were the first in this region of the world to use artillery in land battles. Such weaponry helped them overcome the Mamelukes who had restricted the use of cannons to defending the walls of their large cities. The Mamelukes, renowned as excellent warriors, lost their kingdom due to this strategic error. The Turks took their artillery with them into the battlefield and thereby won the war. In 1516, they completed their conquest of Syria and Palestine and a short while later took Egypt as well. These were the final stages in the establishment of their empire which ruled for approximately 400 years over the entire Eastern Mediterranean basin.

When the Turks rebuilt the walls of Jerusalem, they did not forget this lesson. Even though Jerusalem was at the time only a small provincial town of no great strategic importance and its existing walls were not suited for the deployment of heavy artillery, the Turks placed cannons at the entrance to the Citadel, which played a vital role in the defense of the city. The new walls were built in such a way that firearms could be deployed upon them.

We continue towards the southern edge of the artillery plaza, entering the exterior moat of the Citadel where we see the remains of an ancient quarry and a ritual bath from Second Temple times. Now we reach the entrance to the Ramparts Walk. As we climb the steep iron stairway, we catch our last glimpse of the Citadel. The Turkish minaret, which seems quite small when seen from inside the Citadel, now towers above us in all its glory.

'Kishle' The next section of the Ramparts Walk runs close by Jerusalem's military garrison, which in the course of time became the 'Kishle', the police station and prison of the Old City.

The Turkish word *Kishle* means 'winter palace'. The garrison was built in the 1830s, during the reign of Mohammed Ali and his son Ibrahim Pasha. Mohammed Ali was the Turkish viceroy of Egypt, but, unsatisfied by that title, gathered his forces and in the course of time became its autonomous ruler. In 1831 he began his series of conquests to the north into the very heart of the Ottoman Empire. His son Ibrahim, who commanded his army, conquered Syria and Palestine and pushed on to the Anatolian plateau. It was only under pressure from the European powers and Russia that he was forced to stop his advance. Mohammed Ali pulled back his troops, but was allowed to keep part of the lands he had already conquered, including Syria and Palestine.

During the decade of their rule in Palestine, Mohammed Ali and Ibrahim Pasha initiated a series of reforms in the fields of administration, agriculture, irrigation, transport, industry, etc. This conquest brought with it a period of modernization in Palestine and aroused the interest of the European powers in the development of the country. The projects undertaken by Mohammed Ali and Ibrahim Pasha also left their mark on the physical features of Jerusalem. They renovated the Moslem structures in the vicinity of the Tomb of David, and built army barracks and military installations on the roads, including the Kishle.

The new military garrison was situated near the city's main gate from the west, close to the Citadel, and continued to serve Jerusalem even after the Turks won the city back from the Egyptians. The Turks added a military hospital to the compound. It later served as a police station for the British, for the Jordanians after the Old City fell into their hands in 1948 and since 1967 — for the Israel Police Force.

As we continue on our route, we can see part of the Armenian Quarter inside the city walls. Outside the walls we can see the Hinnom Valley and the neighborhoods located west of the Valley.

The Armenian Quarter From this vantage point, the buildings in the Armenian Quarter are visible from their rear. The empty spaces between this quarter and the city wall are surprisingly extensive. The first compound is that of the Armenian Theological Seminary and alongside it the basketball court used by the seminarians.

The history of the Armenians, who originally came from the mountain regions of eastern Turkey, northern Iraq and the southern region of the former USSR (the present-day Republic of Armenia), is replete with struggles for religious and political autonomy.

The Armenians' unique national character is reflected in the development of an alphabet consisting of 38 signs for their spoken language. As early as the fifth century, Armenian scholars translated the Bible into their language, later adding translations of the Church Fathers. Their church, like other eastern churches such as the Syriac, Coptic and Ethiopian, did not adhere to certain principles of the Christian faith accepted by the heads of the Church in Rome and Byzantium. They remained politically independent and jealously guarded their religious autonomy from the centers of Roman Catholic rule. The fact that the Armenians, like members of the other eastern Christian communities, were under Moslem rule for a number of centuries certainly made it easier for them to preserve their religious autonomy.

76

The Armenian Quarter, the Patriarchate

Armenia maintained its independence in various forms until the fourteenth century. From the mid-fifteenth century it became part of the Ottoman Empire. During the nineteenth century, with their rule on the verge of collapse, the Turks became suspicious of Armenian loyalty; the fact that large concentrations of Armenians lived in areas under Russian domination served to increase Turkish suspicion. The European powers tried to alleviate the Armenians' situation and to defend them from attack by Moslem Kurds. Expressions of Armenian nationalism, at times accompanied by armed uprisings, were brutally suppressed by the Turks. Turkish persecution of the Armenians reached a height during the first year of World War I, as Turks and Russians fought on Armenian soil. The Turks expelled the Armenians living in Turkey, massacring almost one million of them, nearly completely destroying their homeland.

There has been an Armenian community in Jerusalem at least from the fifth century, apparently located then in the same area that it inhabits today. Archeological finds have also revealed the existence of an Armenian community outside the city wall, in the vicinity of Damascus Gate.

The Armenians flourished during the period of Crusader rule in Jerusalem. They assisted the newcomers in their conquest of the Holy Land and developed a special relationship with the Crusad-

77

ers. In fact, relations were so good that at least two of the Crusader kings of Jerusalem took wives from this community. Even the possibility of uniting the Armenian and Catholic churches was explored. During this period, the material condition of the Armenian community in Jerusalem improved greatly, as it apparently received generous monetary contributions from the Crusader-Armenian royal families.

One expression of this community's wealth was the church it erected during the Crusader period. The building, easily recognizable by its octagonal dome, is one of the most beautiful churches to have survived from that time. It is dedicated to two saints both bearing the name of James. The first is St. James 'the Lesser', sometimes also alluded to as the 'brother of Jesus'.

James 'the Lesser' was the first leader of Jerusalem's Christian community. Very little is known about this saint; the Armenians believe that his house was situated on the site of the present church. The second saint was known as James 'the Greater', one of the twelve Apostles appointed by Jesus to spread his teachings. St. James became the first of the Apostles to be martyred; tradition has it that he was executed by order of Agrippas, King Herod's grandson.

From where we are standing, it is difficult to fully appreciate the layout of the Armenian Quarter. It is surrounded by a wall which virtually isolates it from its surroundings. Inside are the buildings of the Armenian Patriarchate, the monks' living quarters, churches, a library, a museum which houses the Patriarchate's treasures (well worth a visit!), a printing press and—of course—dwellings.

Though Jerusalem's Armenian community numbers no more than 3,000 people, it makes a significant contribution to the city's commerce. Armenians throughout the world hold it in special regard; the head of the Jerusalem community holds the title of Armenian Patriarch of Jerusalem. Its status has been greatly enhanced since the establishment in the early 1920s of the Theological Seminary.

The 'Sultan's Pool' The towers on the city wall provide us with a number of points from which we can obtain a good view of the New City. Far below the city wall, the Hinnom Valley spreads before us. Its biblical name is connected with ceremonies conducted here during the First Temple period, at which time sacrifices were offered up to the Canaanite god Moloch. During the Second Temple period the valley was dammed up in order to contain the runoff water which

View to the west: Yemin Moshe Quarter, Mishkenot Sha'ananim, the Hinnom Valley

coursed through it during the winter. The resulting pool was called 'The Pool of the Snakes' and — during the Crusader period — 'Lacus Germani' (the Pool of Germanus) after the nobleman who owned a farm on the valley slope. The pool was restored under the Mamelukes and once again during the Ottoman period, since when it is known as the Sultan's Pool, a reference to the Sultan Suleiman the Magnificent who ordered it renovation. Until the Six-Day War, the area was neglected due to its proximity to the Israel-Jordan armistice line, the danger of mines and of Jordanian snipers stationed on the city wall. In recent years the Sultan's Pool area has been landscaped and on summer evenings concerts and outdoor performances are held there.

79

Yemin Moshe and Mishkenot Sha'ananim

Rows of closely built red-roofed houses are visible atop the west bank of the Hinnom Valley. This is the Yemin Moshe quarter, one of the oldest in Jerusalem's New City. At its southern end are two elongated buildings. This was the first Jewish public housing project to be built outside the Old City walls — Mishkenot Sha'ananim.

The Yemin Moshe neighborhood was established in 1892 on land purchased in 1857 by Sir Moses Montefiore, an English Jewish philanthropist who did much to alleviate the condition of Jews in many parts of the world, and named after him. The neighborhood was built and settled by a joint association of Ashkenazi and Sephardi Jews. It suffered heavy damage during the War of Independence, and for years was a slum area along the Israel-Jordan armistice line. Many of the veteran residents left the quarter, being replaced by new immigrants. In the late 1960s, after the Six-Day War, the majority of the area's inhabitants sold their houses and moved to other parts of the city. The neighborhood, which has known many ups-and-downs since it was first established at the end of the nineteenth century, was painstakingly renovated and has become a luxury quarter.

The adjacent structures — Mishkenot Sha'ananim — underwent a similar process. The buildings were erected by Sir Moses Montefiore in 1860 with financial assistance from the estate of Judah Touro, a New Orleans Jewish philanthropist. The first building was to serve as a model for dwellings outside the Old City walls. Planned by an English architect, at first it contained twenty living units, outhouses, water cisterns, a neighborhood oven and two synagogues — one each for Ashkenazi and Sephardi Jews. Like Yemin Moshe, erected afterwards, Mishkenot Sha'ananim was designed to accommodate members of both Jewish communities. Units were allocated to poor families who drew lots, but there was also no dearth of the well-to-do who did not have to rely on luck to obtain accommodation there.

This old neighborhood flourished again after the Six-Day War. The veteran residents were provided with alternate housing in other parts of the city, the buildings were renovated and turned into living quarters for official guests of the City of Jerusalem. Famous authors, scholars, musicians and artists are invited to stay here, to be imbued with Jerusalem's unique atmosphere and create works which exemplify the inspiration that Jerusalem has to offer.

Above Yemin Moshe stands a windmill, erected by Montefiore as a means of livelihood for the area's new residents. The windmill functioned for only a short time before going out of commission. Today it houses a small exhibition depicting the life of Sir Moses Montefiore and his efforts on behalf of the city of Jerusalem. A reconstruction of his famous carriage is on display in the courtyard.

The King David Hotel

On the horizon, at the top of the hill, stands Jerusalem's most venerable prestigious hotel — the King David. Established in 1931, it soon gained fame for its sumptuous accommodations and was preferred by leading international personalities who visited Jerusalem. Towards the end of the Mandate period, the hotel had been home to the British Government Secretariat and to the British military GHQ in Palestine. In 1946, the southern wing of the hotel was blown up by members of Irgun Zva'i Leumi, a Jewish underground movement which opposed the continued British rule in Palestine. The bombing was not in keeping with the policy of the leadership of Palestine's Jewish community at the time, and led to a rift among the Jewish defense forces which had then been functioning under a joint leadership. During the late 1960s the hotel was renovated with the addition of two storeys, leaving a telltale 'seam' where the original structure ended.

ount Zion After looking at Yemin Moshe, Mishkenot Sha'ananim and the King David Hotel, we continue our walk atop the city wall, arriving at its southwestern corner. Below us are the restored remains of a tower built by the Moslems who reconquered Jerusalem from the Crusaders. The wall turns eastward, cutting across Mount Zion. Beyond the bend in the wall, a lower wall can be seen enclosing a Roman Catholic cemetery. Behind it is the Armenian cemetery adjoining the now unoccupied Armenian monastery. There are a number of other cemeteries on Mount Zion: Protestants, Catholics, Jews and Moslems — all are buried on its slopes. Some of the cemeteries are beautifully situated, others are nondescript. Some were consecrated as recently as the nineteenth century, while others have been in use for hundreds of years. The forms of burial in each cemetery reflect the nature of each community and the motivation of its members to live in Jerusalem and to be buried there.

In some cemeteries the dead were buried in tiers, one above the other, due to lack of space, while in others they were buried directly in the ground.

Multiplicity of burial grounds is one of Mount Zion's prime characteristics, and for many reasons. The Hinnom Valley and its slopes served as an important burial site during the Second Temple period, with many tombs cut into its limestone cliffs. On the slope of the Hinnom Valley is a site which Christian tradition has identified as Hakel Dama — the 'Field of Blood', a plot of land bought by Judas Iscariot with the pieces of silver he received for betraying Jesus and where he was buried after committing suicide. This tradition turned the valley into a sacred burial site for European Christian pilgrims who came to Jerusalem and died during their sojourn here.
During the seventh century, Mount Zion began to be associated in Christian tradition with the site where Mary, mother of Jesus, came to rest in eternal sleep. Such traditions undoubtedly were influential in turning Mount Zion

into a coveted burial place, especially for Christians. As we learned while observing the Mount of Olives, Jews preferred to be buried on the city's eastern side, while the Moslems preferred the eastern and northern sides of the city. However, there were Jews, especially among the poor, as well as Karaites and Moslems, who were buried on the slopes of Mount Zion and in the Hinnom Valley. This certainly cannot be attributed to the tradition connected with Mary, nor do other reasons, such as the proximity to the Tomb of David, provide a satisfactory explanation. It would appear that the reason was primarily geographic, as this region was close to the residential areas and was easily accessible. For a number of centuries it was entirely uninhabited and was thus readily usable as a burial site.

Mount Zion is dotted with sites sacred to Christians, Jews and Moslems. The first such site on our route belongs to the Armenians. Near the Armenian cemetery is an abandoned monastery dedicated to Caiaphas, the High Priest at the time of the trial of Jesus. (His family tomb has recently been discovered in archeological excavations near Government House.) Armenian tradition has it that this was the site of Caiaphas' house, where Jesus was brought before he was handed over to the Romans. There was also a garden on the premises. The Armenians intend to build a new church here and in fact began construction in the early 1970s; foundations were laid and construction of the church and belltower begun. However, completion has been delayed due to lack of funds. Archeological excavations carried out here in 1971 uncovered a house dating to the end of the First Temple period and a Second Temple period dwelling with basements and wall frescoes, as well as remnants of a paved Byzantine street.

'Tomb of David' and the Cenacle Beyond the far side of the Armenian compound we can see two large building complexes: one includes the 'Tomb of David', the Cenacle and some of the buildings of the 'Diaspora Yeshiva'. The second is larger, but of less historical significance. This is the German Catholic Church of the Dormition, a large beautiful building distinguished by its pointed dome and belltower topped by a weather vane, which commands the southern horizon.

Popular tradition identifies this location with the tomb of King David. Numerous legends have glorified the site and recounted the miracles that occurred here. Supplicants, mystics and pilgrims of all religious persuasions have been attracted to the spot.

The building known as the 'Tomb of David' has throughout centuries been the focus of many hallowed traditions, which apparently originated during the Byzantine period. A spacious Byzantine church here commemorated Jerusalem's early Christian community, at the very end of the Second Temple

82

period. In fact, this was the world's first organized Christian community anywhere, and its members lived on Mount Zion. The Byzantine church was called 'Hagia Zion', i.e. 'Holy Zion', as well as 'Mother of All Churches'. It was destroyed and another built on its ruins by the Crusaders who, in characteristic fashion, tied many legends to this church. One earlier tradition, dating from the tenth century, identifies the site with that in which King David was buried. The handful of Jews living in Jerusalem at the time were not inclined to accept these traditions, but after the Crusaders were expelled from the city and Jews returned and settled on Mount Zion, they too began to believe in this tradition relating to King David's burial place.

Another tradition, which gained hold during the Crusader period, designated the room on the second floor of the Crusader Church of Zion as the scene of the Last Supper. And so, varying traditions were concentrated around the same building: the Judeo-Christian identification of the site as the tomb of King David and the Christian tradition identifying the upper floor of the same building as the place where Jesus held the last festive supper with his disciples. Another Christian tradition claims that it was here that the Holy Spirit descended upon Jesus' disciples and caused them to prophesy in seventy languages.

The Jewish and Christian traditions connected to this site proved fateful for both religious communities. During the fourteenth century, relations between them became more charged, with the arrival of a new Catholic Christian community; the Franciscan monks built their monastery on Mount Zion near David's Tomb. The monastery courtyard still survives and today constitutes the entrance plaza to the Tomb of David.

Since the altercations between the Jewish community and the Franciscan monks proved unresolvable by compromise, the Mameluke rulers found it necessary to decide which side would retain the rights to the holy site. There are records surviving from the fifteenth century — letters written by heads of the Franciscan Monastery to the Pope, accusing the Jews of attempting to bribe the Mameluke officials to transfer control of the Chapel of the Holy Spirit from the Franciscans to the Jews. According to historical evidence, the Jewish 'plot' was unsuccessful; in 1428 the Mameluke rulers confiscated the Tomb of David, turning it into a Moslem place of worship. In retaliation, the Pope issued a decree prohibiting ships of the Kingdom of Naples and the Republic of Venice, the major naval powers in the eastern Mediterranean at the time, from carrying Jewish pilgrims or even transporting goods belonging to Jews living in the Sultan's territories.

In 1452, the Mameluke Sultan ordered the destruction of the chapel built by the Christians above the Tomb of David, even though only a few years earlier permission had been granted the Christians to renovate their church and to use it for services. This time the Jews were not involved, its fate having been sealed by the purely internal considerations of the Mameluke rulers. The Franciscans were expelled from Mount Zion, while the Jews of this period also preferred to live in the present-day Jewish Quarter within the city walls. The Tomb of David and the Cenacle (the Room of the Last Supper) remained under Moslem control until the War of Independence in 1948.

Following Israel's War of Independence, the Tomb of David once more became a site holy to Jews. From 1948 to 1967 it was an object of pilgrimage, being the most sacred Jewish site on Israeli territory, from which it was possible to view the Old City.

The Church of the Dormition

It was here, according to Christian tradition (a relatively late one, dating from the seventh century) that Mary, Mother of Jesus, fell into eternal sleep. The site became most important to Catholics, although less so than the adjacent Room of the Last Supper and the Chapel of the Holy Spirit.

The construction of the Church of the Dormition complex was begun in 1906 and completed in 1910. The magnificent church and the Benedictine abbey next to it are majestic structures in the rounded Byzantine-Romanesque style, thus accounting for their humped external appearance. Atop the belltower is a cock-shaped weather vane, similar to those found in Europe.

The German Catholics were particularly interested in acquiring the Room of the Last Supper, but confidential enquiries carried out by the German Consul in Jerusalem revealed beyond doubt that the site was not for sale. The Tomb of David, situated in that very building, was of such historical and religious

The Dormition Abbey, with the Armenian cemetery in the foreground and the incomplete Armenian church on the left

value to the Moslems, that if the Sultan were to have granted the Christians rights to the site, he would have been in danger of undermining the stability of his regime. The Germans, therefore, decided to purchase only the site of the Dormition. Although the Moslems attributed but little importance to this site, the transaction was nevertheless carried out indirectly, to prevent the price being raised exorbitantly. Accordingly, the Governor of Jerusalem acquired the plot on behalf of the Sultan and transferred it to the Germans, who paid its purchase price.

The transfer of ownership was completed after Kaiser Wilhelm II had set out on his journey to Palestine, and during his visit a short but impressive public ceremony was held to mark the event. On Monday, October 31, 1898, the land on which the Church and Abbey of the Dormition were to be erected was transferred to German Catholic ownership.

Zion Gate Zion Gate is also called 'Bab Harat al-Yahud' ('Jewish Quarter Gate') in Arabic because of its proximity to the Jewish Quarter. A fifteenth-century pilgrim, Moses Basola, records that the key to the gate was held by Jews. Another Arabic name was 'Bab al

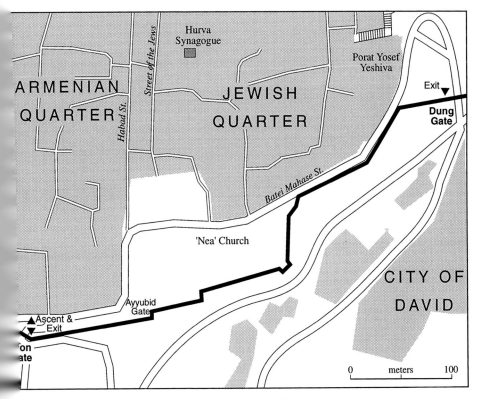

Map 6: From Zion Gate to the Dung Gate

Nebi Da'ud' (the Prophet David's Gate), since it provided access from the Old City to the Tomb of David.

In ancient times there was no gate on this site. In the Second Temple period, and probably during the late First Temple period, Mount Zion was included within the city precincts. The same holds true for the Byzantine period, when the Church of Zion was one of the city's largest and most beautiful. It would seem that Mount Zion was first outside the city bounds in the eleventh century, even prior to the Crusader conquest in 1099. During the Crusader period, there were a gate and a postern in the wall here to ease passage from the Old City to Mount Zion, on which the majestic Crusader church stood. There are some who claim that the Crusaders refortified Mount Zion and, indeed, some of the illustrations which have survived from the Middle Ages clearly show these fortifications. The Moslems, who conquered the city from the Crusaders, built a larger and more imposing gate several score meters to the east.

The Zion Gate's importance, therefore, did not derive from topographical factors. Unlike the Damascus or Jaffa Gates, it is situated on an easily accessible topographical route. Its location and importance were determined over the centuries by changing political-economic decisions as to whether Mount Zion should be within the city wall or should most of it be left outside. When Mount Zion was not within the city wall, a gate was required to provide access from the city to the places of worship of the various religious communities remaining on Mount Zion.

During the War of Independence, it was through the Zion Gate, the closest point of access from West Jerusalem to the Jewish Quarter, that an unsuccessful Israeli attempt was made to save the Jewish Quarter from conquest by the Jordanian Arab Legion. From November 29, 1947, the day on which the United Nations General Assembly passed a resolution which decided to partition Palestine into two states—one Jewish and the other Arab, the Jewish Quarter was besieged and cut off from the rest of the city. On May 19, 1948, a platoon of the Palmah (the elite self-defense units of the pre-state Jewish community in Palestine), commanded by David Elazar, succeeded in placing explosives at the entrance to the gate and advancing into the Jewish Quarter, thus creating an opportunity to rescue its inhabitants. One day earlier, the Palmah had taken Mount Zion. The platoon was not strong enough to hold the Quarter and relieve its defenders. When it was forced to retreat, and no other reinforcements came to their assistance, the fate of the Jewish Quarter's residents was sealed. It fell to the Jordanian forces and its residents taken prisoner. However, the Arab Legion did not succeed in wresting Mount Zion from Jewish control and it remained in Israeli territory. A short account of the battle has been recorded on a stone inscription affixed to the wall inside the Zion Gate's gatehouse:

> On the evening preceding Tuesday the 9th of Iyar 5708, May 18th, 1948, members of the Harel Palmah unit conquered Mount Zion. The next day, before sunrise, they broke through Zion Gate. Twenty-two

Zion Gate

fighters rushed to the aid of the courageous defenders of the Jewish Quarter; bereft of tanks and artillery, they risked their lives to guard the walls of Jerusalem. Those passing through this gate shall remember them.

The road just inside the wall runs parallel to it for a few dozen meters and then turns in a northerly direction. The turret opposite the curve in the road is situated on the medieval site of Zion Gate. This ancient gate was the southern end of the main street — the Cardo — that ran the length of Jerusalem from north to south during the Roman-Byzantine period.

e Cardo While standing atop the Damascus Gate we saw the northern end of the Cardo and learned that the main streets traversing today's Old City were laid during the Roman-Byzantine period.

87

The Byzantine Cardo, which was a wide and well-appointed street, has served since then as the basis for the main passage between the north and south sections of the city. The main street transecting the breadth of the city from east to west is still built on the route of the Byzantine Decumanus. Over the years, however, these routes have been widened and undergone functional changes.

Not all of Jerusalem's many rulers have been interested in maintaining the 'grand plan' of these roads; probably even those who had been able to impose their will upon the city's inhabitants were unprepared to maintain the wide Byzantine boulevards. Thus the Cardo was divided up into narrower sections, thereby increasing its commercial and residential potential. Two parallel streets — Hayehudim St. and Habad St. — run today along the route of the Cardo's southern section.

The ancient Zion Gate, above which we are standing, did not exist in the Byzantine period. The city then extended along the slopes of Mount Zion and there was no need for a gate (although some scholars claim that as early as the Roman period an internal wall already existed here). It seems that the gate was built in the first period of Moslem rule, when the city's population greatly diminished, the slopes of Mount Zion were no longer populated and a wall separated this area from the rest of the city. The Crusaders continued to use this gate, probably built by their Moslem predecessors, as the passage to Mount Zion. The Ayyubid Moslem rulers — descendants of Saladin — restored the city wall after they reconquered Jerusalem from the Crusaders and built a tower on the site. Their restoration work was commemorated in a monumental inscription discovered among the remains of the Ayyubid tower in archeological excavations carried out here. It is of interest to note that this Ayyubid tower was destroyed shortly after it was restored, indeed by the very people who constructed it.

The Ayyubids, who at first feared that they might have to hand over Jerusalem to their Crusader enemies, fortified the city and renovated its walls. When they later became convinced that all notwithstanding, the Crusaders would still take the city, the Ayyubids preferred to tear down the walls, thus forcing the new conquerors to defend an open city, difficult to protect effectively.

As it turned out, the city did eventually fall to the Crusaders, who did not even attempt to restore its walls. Neither did the

Crusader remains in the southern garden of the Jewish Quarter

Mamelukes, who ruled the city at a later stage. Experts on the Mameluke period claim that the principal reason for this oversight was fear of the Crusaders' return. Thus the medieval Zion Gate was never rebuilt and eventually forgotten. When the Ottoman Turks rebuilt the present city wall, they provided it with the present gate leading to the slopes of Mount Zion.

Extensive archeological excavations were carried out opposite the tower, under which the remains of the ancient tower were discovered The area was originally intended to serve as an underground parking lot for the residents of the newly-restored Jewish Quarter. However, Israeli law requires that excavations be carried out within any area defined as an archeological site before construction is begun. The law is intended to ensure the scientific examination of any remains prior to their being covered up or ruined forever. Excavations on this site uncovered, among other finds, a large Crusader building and a Byzantine church. The area has been landscaped and turned into an archeological garden open to the public.

On the other side of the archeological garden is an open parking lot and beyond that we can see the buildings of the Jewish Quarter.

The Jewish Quarter From our present observation point it is not possible to view the inside of the Jewish Quarter; only the walls of its closest buildings are visible. We warmly suggest that the Quarter's restored byways be visited after completing the Ramparts Walk.

The origins of settlement in the Jewish quarter have not yet been determined and experts are divided as to when the Jewish community first began to congregate in this area. There was a small Jewish community in Jerusalem during the Crusader period, but the exact area in which it resided is uncertain. According to a Jewish traveller who visited Jerusalem during the 1270s, the Jews lived near the Tower of David. For some time it was believed that the beginnings of the Jewish Quarter lay in the visit to Jerusalem in 1267 of Moses ben Nahman (Nahmanides, known in Hebrew by his acronym, Ramban), an important rabbinic personality from abroad. Other scholars claim that a Jewish neighborhood began to take shape during the fourteenth or fifteenth centuries. However, it is universally accepted that by the end of the Mameluke period, at the beginning of the sixteenth century, at least 200 Jewish families lived in this neighborhood.

A variety of reasons accounted for the growth of the Jewish community in Jerusalem at this time. Following the expulsion of Jews from Spain in 1492 and the Ottoman conquest of Palestine in 1517, the number of Jewish inhabitants of the city increased and their standard of living improved. It was then that economic and social hegemony passed from the veteran Jewish inhabitants of the city, who had lived there under the Mamelukes, to the newly-arrived Spanish Jews. The latter enhanced Jewish involvement in Jerusalem's economy; indeed, since then Jews have been well-represented in the city's marketplaces. By the middle of the sixteenth century there were no less than 324 Jewish property owners. One indication of the growth of the city's Jewish population, and especially of the Sephardi community, was the establishment at the end of the sixteenth century of a number of new Sephardi synagogues—the Yohanan Ben Zakkai Synagogue, the Elijah Synagogue, the Istambuli Synagogue and others.

During the seventeenth and the beginning of the eighteenth centuries, a wave of Ashkenazi Jews from Europe arrived in Jerusalem. Two concentrations developed at this time in the Jewish Quarter: the Sephardi center that developed around the Yohanan Ben Zakkai Synagogue complex, and the 'Ashkenazi Compound'—a plot of land that had belonged since the fifteenth century to Jews of Ashkenazi origin. The arrival of Rabbi Judah 'the Hassid' and his entourage in 1700 considerably increased the size of the Ashkenazi community, but not to the point that it became dominant. Soon after Rabbi Judah's arrival, the Ashkenazi community sank deeply into debt and was forced to leave the city for a prolonged period.

During the nineteenth century, the Jewish Quarter of Jerusalem flourished once again. Part of Safed's Jewish community moved south to Jerusalem, spurred by the outbreak of an epidemic in the Galilee and by a severe earthquake. The Egyptian conquest of the city, which continued throughout the 1830s, brought in its wake prosperity, and the immigration of Jews from all over Europe. Especially important was the arrival of disciples of the Lithuanian rabbinic sage, Rabbi Elijah of Vilna, beginning in the first decade of the nineteenth century. All these led to the establishment of synagogues, religious seminaries, public institutions, hospitals, postal services, etc. By mid-century the Quarter contained 23 synagogues belonging to various

The Jewish Quarter before its destruction in 1948

Ruins of the Tiphereth Israel Synagogue, destroyed during the War of Independence

communities; in 1875 Jerusalem counted 15,000 Jewish inhabitants. With the establishment of Jewish neighborhoods outside the city wall, the Jewish population within the Old City diminished. This gradual Jewish exodus to areas outside the walls continued throughout the first half of the twentieth century, so that by the eve of the War of Independence only 1,700 Jews remained in the Old City, mainly the elderly and ailing.

During the War of Independence, the residents of the Jewish Quarter fought a valiant battle for their very existence, until they were overpowered in May 1948. The Quarter fell to the Jordanian Arab Legion, its defenders were taken captive, and the rest of its inhabitants transferred to the New City. It was not until after the Six-Day War of 1967 that Jews began to live in the Old City once more. In April 1968, the Jewish Quarter Development Corporation was established; its complex goal has been to revive and resettle the Quarter, while maintaining its unique character. The planners faced a tremendous challenge: to evacuate the people then residing in the area, find them alternative accommodation and pay them compensation, and then restore the neighborhood's ancient buildings, part of which were in ruins and others badly damaged by dampness. The many sites upon which new buildings were due to be built had first to undergo archeological excavation. The amazing discoveries found under the foundations of the structures necessitated changes in the original plans Architects and project planners were often required to forgo the use of basements and ground floors. Some of the archaelogical remains have been restored and opened to visitors.

Furthermore, the construction process of itself was not an easy one. Building contractors were required to erect most unique structures, it being almost impossible to use architectural plans for more than one building. In many of the buildings, each window is different from the others. Transportation difficulties within the Quarter forced contractors to resort to the age-old means of donkeys to haul immense quantities of construction materials and equipment. The construction effort is now by and large completed; it is now possible to wander through the Jewish Quarter's unique architectural complexity and see at first-hand the original solutions devised to overcome most of the problems originally faced by the planners.

St. Peter in Gallicantu Looking outwards from the city wall, we can spot one of Jerusalem's most interesting twentieth-century churches, the Church of St. Peter in Gallicantu ('St. Peter at Cockcrow'). According to Catholic tradition, this is the site of the house of the High Priest Caiaphas, to which Jesus was brought from Gethsemane. As already noted, the Armenians believe the House of Caiaphas to be located in the Armenian Garden that we saw earlier on our walk, but in this, as in many other contexts, each Christian community maintains its own traditions and determines the location of its own holy sites.

The Catholics erected this church to commemorate an event that occurred after Jesus' arrest, but which he had prophesied earlier, while still at liberty. The New Testament relates that Jesus' disciples refused to acknowledge him after his arrest, denying even that they recognized him. Three times did Peter, his

Part of the Jewish Quarter before its destruction in 1948

loyal disciple, deny Jesus before sunrise, before the cock crowed (*gallicantu* in Latin) three times at sunrise. The Church was consecrated in the early 1930s and is famous both for the frescoes on its outer walls and for the fact that the archeological excavations carried out on this site during the nineteenth century were among the first in Jerusalem's history.

The Nea Church We continue in an easterly direction until we reach a corner tower. The wall turns left here, towards the north. Extensive archeological excavations conducted here during the 1970s exposed the remains of a large Byzantine church, dating to 543. It was then known as the New Church of Mary, or simply as 'the Nea' (new, in Greek).

This church was considered at the time of its construction to be the largest and most exquisite of all churches in Jerusalem. A contemporary historian described it as an incomparable 'sanctuary'. Despite its huge dimensions and magnificent construction it was utterly destroyed at the end of the Byzantine era, leaving hardly any vestiges. The Nea's location became a hotly-debated topic among historians of Jerusalem, but archeological excavations have at last provided indisputable proof. Several sections of the Nea church and of the monastery that existed alongside it have been uncovered. A large dedicatory inscription, attesting to the fact that this was indeed the missing Nea Church, was found in a huge vaulted and arched water cistern beneath the monastery.

The Jerusalem municipality decided to preserve these impressive remains while exploiting the site's magnificent view to the east. Plans were drawn up to build an open-air theater with the city wall serving as a stage and the archeological remains situated beneath the seats. However, objections were raised, leading to modification of the plans. An impressive archeological garden, which can be seen from the ramparts, was developed on the site instead.

The City of David At the bottom of the slope outside the city wall is an offshoot of the Kidron Valley, which bisects the city and serves as the Old City's main transportation artery. Over the centuries the riverbed has filled up with silt so that it is no longer possible to estimate its original depth. During the Second Temple period, before the blockage occurred, it was known as the 'Tyropoean'. On the further, eastern side of the valley is a low hill called 'The City of David'; this was the nucleus of ancient Jerusalem. Beyond this point, to the east, the deep bed of the Kidron Valley can be discerned with little effort.

94

At the bottom of the valley is the Gihon Spring, which was the main water source for the city's inhabitants in ancient times, and was probably one of the factors determining Jerusalem's location in the first place. From this relatively high and distant vantage point, we can envisage the entire scope of the biblical city of Jerusalem and understand how truly small it was. The hill is called 'The City of David' because this was the site that King David conquered from the Jebusites and which he turned into the capital of his kingdom.

The city, which had been founded many generations prior to King David's conquest, expanded steadily; it would appear that even during the First Temple period this small eastern hill had already become overcrowded. Thus, even though no source of water other than the Gihon was available in the city's environs, some of the inhabitants moved to the western hill, part of which, now called Mount Zion, is today outside the city wall, while the other section remains inside it, in what are now the Armenian and Jewish Quarters.

Jerusalem continued to expand. During the Second Temple period, most of the city was to be found on the western hill and its slopes. The Romans were the first to completely abandon the eastern hill; during their rule of the city, it was confined to the summit of the western hill. True, when the population increased substantially during the Byzantine era, the city expanded once more to encompass the City of David, but from the Crusader period onwards it was confined mainly to the territory within its wall. The eastern hill became virtually uninhabited and was resettled only during the course of the twentieth century.

On the skyline we can see some of the mountains surrounding Jerusalem. To the south our view is bounded by the 'Hill of Evil Counsel', topped by a large white building with a flag waving above it. This is Government House, built by the British Mandatory authorities as the residence of the British High Commissioner in Palestine. Since 1948, it is the headquarters of United Nations truce supervisors and peacekeeping forces in the Middle East.

To the east lies a hill capped by a monastery which is, in turn, surrounded by a thick grove of pine trees. Some identify this as the 'Mount of Corruption' mentioned in the Book of Kings as the site where King Solomon built altars to the idols of Moab and Ammon; hence its name.

he Dung Gate Descending a bit further along the city wall, we come to the Dung Gate. To the left, inside the wall, we see the buildings of the restored Jewish Quarter. To the right, outside the city wall, we can view the archeological garden, mentioned above, which was laid out close to the wall upon completion of the excavations here. Just a few meters before the present gate, an ancient gate tower dating back to the Crusader and Ayyubid periods has been uncovered.

Dung Gate after renovation. Only the ornamental upper arch remains of the original passageway

The name Dung Gate is first mentioned in the Book of Nehemiah: "But the dung gate repaired Malchiah ... he built it, and set up the doors thereof, the locks thereof and the bars thereof." At that time the gate was apparently situated south of its present location. Its name indicates its original purpose. In ancient times the city's refuse was removed through the gate, for leaving it inside was forbidden due to the city's sacredness. Jewish tradition has it that: "Ten things have been said of Jerusalem... no refuse is to be within it." The gate area also served as the site where tanners and other craftsmen plied their trades. It was through the Dung Gate that the residents went to the Gihon and Ein Rogel springs to bring water into the city.
The Arab name of the gate, 'Gate of the Maghrebites', refers to the Moslems from North Africa (the Maghreb) who inhabited the neighborhood facing the Western Wall. During the Middle Ages it was called 'Bab Silwan' since a road leads from this gate down to the pool of Silwan.

The Ottoman-period Dung Gate was built much in the same manner as were the other gates of the city: the entrance approach was not direct, as it is today, but rather at an angle, in order to prevent rapid, uninterrupted entry into the city. It was also the smallest of all the gates. Under Jordanian rule, the barrier was demolished and the gate widened, as was done to the Lions' Gate and Herod's Gate, in order to provide access to vehicular traffic. This gate was again renovated in 1985. Just across the street, within the wall, is another important site — the Ophel archeological excavations. Here have been revealed the approaches and the surroundings of the Temple Mount, the site of the First and Second Temples. (The site is open to visitors on Sunday through Fridays from 7 AM to 7 PM; there is an entrance fee.)

Temple Mount The Temple Mount is encompassed by massive walls, tens of meters high. Until the beginning of excavations in 1968, these walls were to a great extent covered by rubble and refuse. The excavations have revealed the magnitude and majesty of the walls that once surrounded the mount; they have also uncovered the entrances and exits of the Temple Mount itself.

While we have become used to the term 'Temple Mount', it is difficult to discern that it is in fact a hill. From our vantage point we can see only high walls from behind which two domes protrude: a small one at the southern extremity of the 'mount', that of al-Aqsa Mosque, the central mosque of Jerusalem's Moslem community, and the larger, golden 'Dome of the Rock', built over the rock which, in Second Temple times, stood before the Holy of Holies, and is also the site from which, according to Moslem tradition, Mohammed ascended to heaven. The high walls sur-

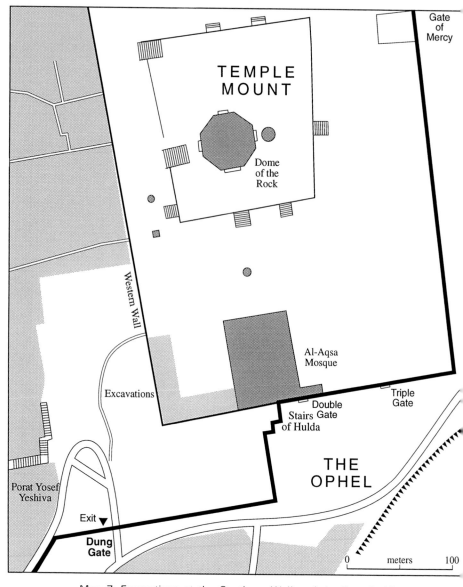

Map 7: Excavations at the Southern Wall and the Temple Mount

rounding the Temple Mount conceal from our view what is taking place inside. In order to enter the sacred compound one must ascend a gradual man-made incline, leading to the Gate of the Maghrebites, the main entrance to the Temple Mount.

The Temple Mount is actually the northern section of Jerusalem's eastern ridge. This section was concealed during the Second Temple period by the walls we can see before us. These walls were not intended only to protect the hill's holy sites but to fill an architectural function as well. The area of the hill, on which the Temple stood, was not spacious enough to contain the multitudes who gathered there on the Jewish pilgrimage festivals during the late Second Temple period. It was impossible to expand the public spaces on the mount's summit to provide for larger numbers of pilgrims without expanding the summit itself. The solution found during the Herodian period was to construct massive support walls while on the inside an enormous platform was built for the pilgrims. A system of underground arches was constructed between the walls and the natural bedrock to support this giant platform and also to solve a problem of Jewish ritual law. In ancient times the slopes of the Temple Mount had been used by the city's inhabitants as a cemetery and thus there was fear of ritual impurity as a result of proximity to or contact with the dead. The expansion of the Temple area made it incumbent upon the builders to ensure that the enlarged area would not come into direct contact with the slopes used for burial. Building upon arches created space between the bedrock and the sanctified structures, thereby preventing defilement of the Temple Mount. Multitudes of pilgrims flocked to Jerusalem during the Second Temple period; Jewish records state that hundreds of thousands of Jews came on the three pilgrimage festivals — Passover, Pentecost and the Feast of the Tabernacles. Philo of Alexandria recorded that: "Tens of thou-

The Temple Mount, view from the wall; the excavations in the foreground

sands of Jews from tens of thousands of cities flock to the Temple on each festival, some from the east and west and others from north and south." Other sources indicate that cities throughout Palestine would literally empty out during the pilgrimage festivals.

The massive support walls surrounding the Temple Mount created a problem. The Temple's planners had to provide entry and exit routes for tens of thousands of pilgrims. Herod's engineers were thus required to cope with pedestrian traffic problems characteristic of a modern metropolis, where massive crowds gather and disperse within short periods of time. However, the physical conditions in Jerusalem, in general, and on the Temple Mount in particular, posed problems much more difficult than those faced by most modern institutions.

A stone pier projects from the wall near the southwest corner of the Temple Mount, the remains of a Second Temple period arch. This was part of a stairway leading from the valley at the top of

Robinson's Arch protruding from the Temple Mount wall, and some archeological excavations at the foot of the wall

the Temple Mount. It is known as 'Robinson's Arch', named for American Bible scholar Edward Robinson who discovered it while exploring Jerusalem during the nineteenth century. The stairway's other sections were uncovered in recent archeological excavations.

We begin our tour of the archeological excavations by viewing them from the Crusader tower. Walk directly along the entrance path and then to the left, up steps which lead us to an observation balcony. This balcony and the buildings between it and the Temple Mount wall were erected in the Middle Ages, probably during the Crusader era. The Crusaders converted the Temple Mount into one of their most important centers in Jerusalem and the Crusader king of Jerusalem established his residence in al-Aqsa Mosque.

The European Christian knights did not refer to al-Aqsa Mosque by that name but rather by a biblical appellation, 'Templum Salomonis' (Solomon's Temple), so as to differentiate between this site and the Dome of the Rock which they called 'Templum Domini' (The Lord's Temple). Even after the palace was transferred to its new site, near the Tower of David, the Temple Mount retained its significance for the Crusaders, both as a focus for pilgrims and as the center of the Order of the Knights of the Temple, at that time the leading military force in the Crusader Kingdom. The Templars turned the underground vaults between the upper esplanade and the bedrock into stables and storerooms. This accounts for the name 'Solomon's Stables', an appellation by which some of these vaults are still known.

Excavations at the Southern Wall — the Ophel Garden We descend the stairs from the observation balcony and return to the archeological excavations. The site's restorers planned this descent to reflect a certain reverse historical progression: we begin at the observation platform, built upon Crusader structures which date back to the twelfth century; we proceed downwards through buildings from the first Moslem period (seventh-eighth centuries) to buildings on a lower level dating from the Byzantine period (fifth-sixth centuries); from there we continue to the lowest level of this section of the excavations, containing Second Temple period structures (first century BCE). In the other section of the excavations, outside the city wall, important finds have been uncovered dating to the First Temple period as well. The plethora of findings uncovered in this massive excavation is staggering. We will refer here to but a few of the most important discoveries and limit ourselves to descriptions of the main eras in which buildings were erected in the area southwest of the Temple Mount. Signposts will help us find the way.

101

The Umayyad Palaces

We will examine the excavation sites and their respective periods in the order they are revealed. The first level we come across beneath that of the Crusader period is that of the palaces erected by the Arab Moslem rulers of the Umayyad dynasty. The caliphs of this dynasty repaired the Temple Mount walls and erected the Mount's two most important extant edifices: al-Aqsa Mosque, which already then served as the main prayer house for the city's Moslems, and the Dome of the Rock, built to mark the spot from which Mohammed ascended to heaven.

The Moslem palaces were square buildings constructed around central courtyards. The now-restored arched rooms were situated on the northeast end of the palace courtyard. In all, six large structures, dating to the Umayyad period, have been found. Some were sizable enough to be considered palaces. South of the Western Wall, archeologists have discovered a bath house built for the use of the Umayyad rulers.

Written records refer only to the caliph's palace and so we have no way of knowing the identity of the other palaces' inhabitants. But the palaces and mosques are evidence of the Umayyad rulers' tremendous efforts towards the development of Jerusalem.

The discovery of the Moslem palaces at the southwest end of the Temple Mount was, indeed, a sensational find. Although written evidence did exist regarding a palace belonging to a Moslem caliph that had been built in Jerusalem, no one knew its exact location and it was wrongly associated by many with a structure located in the Citadel courtyard dating from the early Moslem period.

In 638, Jerusalem was conquered by the Moslems. Already in that century they began to hold Jerusalem sacred, and it soon became one of the three cities to which Moslems made pilgrimages. During the second half of that century, control of the Moslem Empire, then taking shape, was seized by a respected family from Mecca, one of whose sons, Uthman, was already ruling as a caliph. This was the first Moslem family to found a dynasty—the Umayyads, who transferred their seat of government to Damascus and also developed Jerusalem as an administrative and religious center. Early in the eighth century, one of the Umayyad rulers, apparently al-Walid I, began construction of the palaces to the south and southwest of the Temple Mount. In most cities that they developed during their first years in power, the Moslems tended to locate their centers of government near places of worship; thus in Jerusalem the caliph's palace was erected adjacent to the city's mosque. From the second floor of the caliph's palace (we are now in one of its wings), there was direct access to the courtyard on the Temple Mount. This was designed not only to facilitate the caliph's entry and exit, but also to stress the link between the military and civil authority, on the one hand, and religious institutions, on the other.

The Byzantine Level The spiraling stairway leads down out of the Umayyad palace to the Byzantine level. Jerusalem's Christian inhabitants, during the Byzantine period, attached little importance to the Temple Mount. Scant reference is made in contemporary written records to construction having taken place on the Mount, and it appears that no Christian buildings were erected there. For the Christian inhabitants of this period, the Temple Mount was but a symbol of the built-up Jerusalem that Jesus saw in his lifetime and which he prophesied would be destroyed and never rebuilt until his Second Coming at the End of Days.

To Christians, the destruction of the Temple Mount was proof of Jesus' prophecy come true, as well as evidence that the Christian faith was superior to Judaism. They therefore intended to perpetuate this destruction and thus point to it as proof of the New Testament's veracity. The Temple Mount was abandoned and seems not to have been rebuilt intentionally throughout the Byzantine era.

The Byzantines, however, displayed quite a different attitude towards the city at large. Though there were some Christians who posited that the entire city should be left in ruins, because Jesus had prophesied the destruction of Jerusalem, and not the Temple alone, the city nevertheless prospered and flourished under Byzantine rule. Masses of pilgrims flocked here from all over the world, its streets were repaved and widened, new churches were built; population density certainly reached one of the highest levels in the city's long history. This prosperity is reflected in the remains of the residential area built at this time to the south of the Temple Mount. The houses and monasteries stood very close to each other, the streets were no more than narrow lanes and the inhabitants drew their water supply from wells and cisterns. Life was most vibrant here at the foot of the desolate walls of the Temple Mount.

The dwellings uncovered here followed a similar plan. Most buildings were built around a small central courtyard and were more than one storey high, the lower floors serving as storerooms and workshops. Since upper floors are always the first to be destroyed, excavations generally expose only the lower service quarters. Such is the case here. The tour route takes us through a residential storey and a basement floor which also served as a water cistern. The floors were paved in mosaics, often ornamented by simple designs. Steep stairways, sometimes hewn out of the bedrock, led from the basement to the upper floors. We will pass through an upper residential floor, a basement floor, a staircase and workshops. Our route finally passes through a hewn-out tunnel below the wall and emerges on the outer side of the Old City wall. Here we can see the vestiges of earlier periods.

As in other areas of this excavation site, early remains from the

First Temple period can be seen alongside vestiges from later periods, Byzantine and Umayyad. The wall is built on top of Umayyad remains, indicating that it dates to a later era, apparently the early Moslem period which predates that of the Crusaders.

The Second Temple Level As we emerge from the tunnel leading from the Byzantine ruins, we see a wide staircase constructed of large stones leading to the Temple Mount wall. These partially restored steps, dating to the Second Temple period, were used by those who came to the Temple. Actually, this is a double staircase. The eastern section, slightly further away from us, leads to a sealed triple gate in the wall. The western section, the wider of the two, also leads up to an entrance in the wall, now blocked by the city wall and by the Crusader buildings abutting on al-Aqsa Mosque.

This double staircase was built during the Second Temple period for the use of pilgrims on their way to the Temple compound. The sealed gates, known as the Hulda Gates, were the main entrances to the Temple plaza.

The source of the name 'Hulda' is undetermined. Some scholars argue that it derives from the tomb of the prophetess Hulda, which was nearby. The distance between the gates is approximately 70 meters, with a 7-meter wide paved road leading to them. A one-way set of stairs leads to each of the two gates; the pilgrims would enter through the eastern gate, walk round the Temple plaza and leave by the exit gate on the western side.
The two staircases were planned to solve a problem mentioned earlier in reference to Robinson's Arch: how to direct the flow of masses of pilgrims visiting the Temple on the three pilgrimage festivals. It was necessary to provide paths for the tens of thousands of pilgrims and the sacrifices which they bore to the Temple. Provision also had to be made to examine each person entering through the gates and to ensure an uninterrupted flow of visitors. This was the purpose of the two staircases and the gates to which they led. The logic behind this plan was similar to that employed in the design of modern buildings and installations destined to accommodate multitudes of people within a short time: a relatively narrow entrance to control them as they enter and a wider exit to enable the crowds to disperse quickly. Separation of the entrance and exit gates guarantees the free flow of those coming and going without obstructing one another.
The internal vaults of the western Hulda Gate are preserved in the underground halls beneath the floor of al-Aqsa Mosque. The Moslems call these halls 'Ancient al-Aqsa'. This gate was restored during the early Moslem period, the signs of repair being visible on the ornamented lintel.

It is recommended to climb these ancient steps, a memorial of the past; when you reach the top, sit down and take in the view. The City of David, the Kidron Valley, the Hill of Evil Counsel—on which today stands Government House, and—on a clear day—the adjacent Judean Desert, can all be seen from here. Below us are the excavations of the southern wall of the Temple, the Umayyad palaces, Byzantine structures and Second Temple period mansions. We will now visit the southwestern corner of the Temple Mount wall where exciting discoveries have been made.

To do this we must return to the city wall. The archeologists opened up a pair of entrances, unintentionally creating the city wall's eighth gate. We enter the gate that brings us to the large Umayyad palace. Continuing in a westerly direction, we can exit through the opening from the palace immediately opposite the pair of entrances. Even though the gate's southern section has been removed, it can easily be identified. The path leads us northward (to the right), with the wall of the large Umayyad palace to our right.

The Walls of the Temple Mount

This is the best place to examine the manner in which the Temple Mount walls were erected. To the north of the Western (Wailing) Wall, fourteen-meter long ashlars have been found. These stone blocks were cut with the utmost care and were set in place according to a method called 'dry construction'. No cement is required when building with such massive hewn stones; their very weight—dozens of tons—is sufficient to lock them firmly in place. These ashlars were placed one on top of the other. The walls' corners were built in an interlocking system, the wide side of one layer facing southwards and the wide side of those immediately above and below it facing westward. This ensured the stability of the massive walls.

The engineers took still further precautions. Though they left arched spaces within the stone vaults, they feared that the vaults might not hold the weight over a long period of time. They therefore had particularly wide walls built around the Temple Mount, the ashlars being placed in such a manner that the lower ones jutted out slightly, producing a slightly inclining wall. This incline, the size and weight of the ashlars, and the interlocking corner system, together ensured the stability of the walls.

There is a pit several meters deep at the foot of the wall. In the bottom of the pit are a number of giant smashed stone blocks, lying on their sides, covering a street paved with giant flagstones. This street was built during the Second Temple period, together with the huge walls which loom above it. We can thus appreciate the height to which these walls towered above their surroundings.

The Temple Mount walls rose 31 meters above street level, whereas today they are merely 23 meters high.

Jews praying at the Western (Wailing) Wall, early twentieth century

On the upper section of the wall, running along the entire southern edge of the Temple Mount, was the splendid royal portico built by King Herod. It was used for administrative and civil purposes not necessarily connected with Temple ritual, for the Temple served as more than a religious site. It was also an economic, political and civic center of the utmost importance. At the time, this was the largest edifice in the whole of the Roman Empire.

Among the building blocks found on the road dating from the Second Temple period was one which bore a Hebrew inscription. It had fallen from the wall in the area called 'The Hornblower's House'. Historical sources bearing upon the Jewish revolt against the Romans note that from this corner of the Temple Mount wall, the onset of the Sabbath was heralded by the blowing of the Shofar (ram's horn). This stone, found in pieces on the street below, was probably smashed when it fell from the top of the wall. We have no way of knowing precisely when it fell, but it is tempting to make the assumption that this is an actual remnant of the destruction of the Temple Mount wall by the Romans when they conquered Jerusalem in 70 CE. After much soul-searching, Titus ordered the destruction of the Jewish Temple and its walls. Titus' decision proved to be a turning point in the annals of the Jewish people and in the history of Jerusalem.

We continue to walk next to the western wall of the Temple Mount, with the wall built by the Moslems on our left. It we look up, we will once more see the remnants of an arch that once jutted out of the Temple Mount wall—the very 'Robinson's Arch' which we had earlier seen from afar, as we walked the ramparts.

Let us cross over to the southern edge of the Moslem wall and look at its lowest level. There we can see the lowest part of the pilaster to which 'Robinson's Arch' was connected at its western extremity. It can be easily discerned by the four apertures which served as shops (weights, coins and jars were found).

Looking back towards the Temple Mount, we can see a Hebrew inscription with a phrase from the Book of Isaiah (66:14), with a slight change in the text: "And ye shall see it, and your heart shall rejoice, and their [instead of your] bones shall flourish like the tender grass..." From the height of the level on which it was inscribed, it has been dated to the fourth century CE. It may be silent evidence of the hopes of redemption which stirred the breast of a Jew who was enthused by rumors that the emperor Julian 'the Apostate' (so known because he planned to have his empire relinquish the Christian fate and readopt Hellenistic philosophy) intended to rebuild the Jewish temple. However, Julian — who had come to power at the beginning of the seventh decade of the fourth century — was assassinated three years later, and the temple was never rebuilt.

Continue walking along the path until it ends. To the left we can see a huge pit with beautiful stone paving at the bottom. This is a section of a street of the Second Temple period that ran parallel to the walls of the Temple Mount. On our left we see another, deeper, shaft which at one time reached bedrock. Like many others, it was dug by Charles Warren, an officer of the British Engineers, one of the most important researchers in nineteenth-century Jerusalem. Through the shaft which he dug, we are able to look down beyond the level of the Second Temple period street and see the bedrock upon which were laid the foundations of the western supporting wall of the Temple Mount.

POSTSCRIPT

In this guide we have studied some of the sites that can be viewed from the Jerusalem Ramparts Walk. We did not set out to present a systematic outline history of Jerusalem, nor to describe all that can be seen from the city wall. Rather, we selected sites and historical periods which we believe to be both interesting and significant.

Jerusalem is multi-faceted. Its buildings do not impose themselves upon you. The city's uniqueness lies in the atmosphere that imbues it far more than in the physical externalities of its edifices and streets. There are few buildings in Jerusalem which 'must' be seen. However, the atmosphere, the light, the impact of religious and historical experience—these are 'musts'. To be in Jerusalem without encountering them would be as though you had not visited the city at all. So, seek out the special atmosphere, the light and the sights; feel the vitality and majesty of the city walls, the horror of its wars and destruction; sense Jerusalem's sanctity, zealotry and love—and thereby create your own Jerusalem. Now, having seen the city from above, you will no doubt find it easier to discover it from within.

Photo Credits

We gratefully thank the following photographers and institutions for the use of their photos:

Ilan Sztulman 15, 16, 18, 22, 24, 27, 33, 35, 39, 44, 46, 57, 60, 63, 68, 69, 72, 77, 84, 89, 96

Israel Museum, Jerusalem 18 (top), 36, 64, 93, 106

Zoom 18 (bottom)

Baruch Greenberg 20, 28 (bottom), 34 (bottom), 79

Fred Chesnik 21

Jewish National Fund, Jerusalem 26

David Rubinger 28 (top)

Werner Braun 40, 42, 43, 52, 53, 87, 100

Nathan Karp 91 (top)

Tourjeman Post Museum, Jerusalem 91 (bottom)

Joel Fishman 99

Cover photo: Mike Horton